Visiting Time

by

various authors

&

edited by Stewart Ennis and the contributors

Vagabond Voices
Glasgow

First published in November 2019 by
Vagabond Voices Publishing Ltd.,
Glasgow,
Scotland.

ISBN 978-1-913212-00-1

Printed and bound in Poland

Cover design by Mark Mechan

Typeset by Park Reads, parkreads.co.uk

The publisher acknowledges subsidy towards this publication from Creative Scotland

ALBA | CHRUTHACHAIL

For further information on Vagabond Voices, see the website, www.vagabondvoices.co.uk

Contents

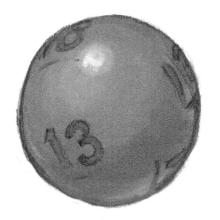

INTRODUCTION

Stewart Ennis

However unusual a prison environment may be, the creative community within it is pretty much like any other. You can find grafters, grifters and blaggers, and the big-hearted, the down-hearted and the broken-hearted. You can find outliers, high fliers, experimenters, the innately talented who make it look sickeningly easy, and those – like most of us – whose gifts are limited but who are smart enough or lucky enough to know how to use to them to best effect. And in this anthology you will find a rich variety of voices and registers. Some confident, some hesitant, some for whom English is a relatively new and tricky second language, and some who are at their maist eloquent scrievin Scots.

I know many of the writers whose work appears in this anthology from my years as Creative Writing lecturer at HMP Shotts. Indeed several of them have been fundamental in bringing this entire project to fruition. Others have moved on, some are still there and some have passed away. A few of them have already seen their work in print thanks to organizations and publications such as *The Koestler Trust, English PEN, The Scottish Book Trust, Inside Times, Snapshots* and of course, the award-winning homegrown *STIR Magazine*, all of which offer prisoners that thing that is so vital to all writers, a platform for their writing.

Then there are those other, less obvious, but equally important writing platforms such as the Royal Conservatoire of Scotland's annual devised theatre week, not forgetting the creative writing courses run by that most wonderful institution, *The Open University*, fifty-years-old this year, of which I too am a beneficiary. I'm pleased to see this book published by Vagabond Voices, who have a reputation for publishing high quality stories, poems, rants and plays, all of which appear between the covers of *Visiting Time*.

People often write about where they are and what they know, and so it should come as no surprise that *Visiting Time* explores various aspects of prison life. However, you will be sorely disappointed if you are hoping to read exclusively about prison. Yes, you will find straight forward unambiguous accounts of life behind bars, cries in the dark, howls at the moon, laughter in the face of adversity, ruminations on remorse, rants and rages against the machine. But just as many are acts of pure imagination: allegorical tales, satires, fairy stories and absurdist experiments that, if they explore ideas of crime and punishment at all, do so in ways that are not immediately obvious. In other words, they are writing about the things that writers have been writing about since they first scratched out words on clay and stone. They are using all the raw material of storytelling at their disposal to find meaning in life, to make sense of it all, or simply and most generously, to entertain and amuse. Yes, sometimes that means they have drawn from the well of their own lived experiences, but at other times they have drawn from those much deeper wells, of observation and imagination.

Having work read by others is important to all writers whether they are prisoners or not. Those others may be total strangers or fellow writers, or they may be friends and family. For some prisoners, having work read, can serve another function; the opportunity to be seen in a different light, to take on an identity other than that of "prisoner". It's a fantastic feeling to get positive feedback from anonymous peers who are judging you solely on the quality of your writing, but it can also be a great source of pride and satisfaction for prisoners to receive feedback from close family and friends, along the lines of, *I didn't know you were a poet, How long have you been a song writer? You should have your stories published? I read that story to your daughter and she loved it. There's more to you than meets the eye.* Eventually, hopefully, that person may feel greater confidence in themselves and in their ability to understand others.

My time as Creative Writing lecturer at HMP Shotts was one of the most rewarding and creative periods in my career. I met some inspiring people there. In every class, bar none, words were written or spoken, that kindled the imagination and set the creative synapses flickering. At its best the creative writing class was a dynamic, supportive and respectful space. It was a place of curiosity, rumbustiousness and occasional irreverence, where people came to explore and ask questions, and where there was no single correct answer. A creative class should be a place where ideas – silly or sensible, for who can tell at first? – are thrown around the room like spaghetti. Some stick, and some slide down the wall and are thrown back into the pot to cook a little longer. No ideas are wasted. All ideas are up for grabs by anyone who happens to be in the vicinity. Throwaway lines that the writer believed "stupid" or "nothing special" often find themselves a new home in a new story, or in someone else's story. Everyone is adding to the great "ocean of notions".

"For a long time now, I have simply tried to write the best I can. Sometimes I have good luck and write better than I can."

Ernest Hemingway in *The Paris Review*, 1954

Such good luck did indeed occur. At its best I came away feeling invigorated and buzzing with ideas (I sincerely hope others did too, at least some of the time). Looking over the contributions to this anthology, I am reminded of the extraordinary creative minds at work during those classes. It should be remembered that being creative in a prison can be enormously challenging. I don't want to linger on this, for this book above all is about the writing, but a little context and perspective won't go amiss. For many, the endless sleepless nights caused by poor mental health, family issues, addictions and goodness knows what else, made getting out of bed for a nine-o'clock in the morning, creative-writing class a real challenge. On more than one occasion the sound of pens scribbling or keyboards rattling was interrupted by a loud snore or a thud as a knackered insomniac nodded off and his head hit the table.

And that may be one reason why many of the pieces in this book are short, very short, almost no more than fragments and fleeting thoughts, barely caught on paper before they disappeared into the ether. That said, there is a great tradition of succinct fiction and terse verse; flash fiction and the haiku being two examples. In any case the fact that some, despite finding it painful to do so, were able to drag themselves out of bed, and then drag a pen across the page and capture those most fleeting of thoughts, was quite an achievement, and indicates the kind of resilience that any writer would value. Of course, insomnia is not the only hurdle to overcome. There is also the self-doubt experienced by all writers at one time or another. Sometimes though (and perhaps this is what Hemingway meant by luck), the untrained hand is smarter than the untrained eye thinks it is, and many is the time that a writer in class has been unable to see the value of his own writing. Although, when you consider how many prisoners went through primary and secondary school being told over and over, *You are useless*, until cowed and humiliated they learned to believe it, this should come as no surprise.

But it is important to add that there was laughter too, and you will find much of that humour in *Visiting Time*. And not just of the gallows variety, but the honest to goodness light-hearted and playful kind. For let's not forget that playfulness is also an important instrument in the writers' toolkit. I am reminded of a fairly recent Scottish prison documentary, where everyone was filmed in brooding close-up and every scene was bathed in dark droning music. The overall effect was one of relentless intensity and gloomy portentousness.

Yes, sometimes it can be like that. But not *all* the time. Where was the laughter? Where was the playfulness? Interestingly, at exactly the same time that this documentary was being broadcast, some prisoners in HMP Shotts were busy singing and dancing to Kylie Minogue's *I Should Be So Lucky*, during a rehearsal for the Christmas show that they'd soon be performing to the children of prisoners. It's a pity that something like that didn't make it into the documentary, it may have balanced the books a little.

The creative writing class was never toiling away in isolation. The staff in the prison Learning Centres are all extremely dedicated, talented, humane and creative people, and all of the work that was done in the English, art, music, maths, literacy, modern studies, and all the other classes – together with the vital work of the library and the various cross curriculum projects – in their own way, directly and indirectly supported and fed into the work in the creative-writing class. Like Scottish education in general, the prison learning centre maintains a broad curriculum, which in turn encourages a broad mind, not unhelpful in creative writing.

"Prisons and their inmates have too real an existence not to have a profound effect on people who remain free."

Jean Genet, *Miracle of the Rose,* 1946

It has to be said that most people – certainly most politicians – are unlikely ever to be seen marching up and down the street chanting, "Better Education for Prisoners". That's a pity. Perhaps they should. These are our prisons, and for reasons too numerous – and, I would hope, too obvious – to mention, we should take an interest in what goes on inside them.

Finally a message to the writers; your work is now out in the world and has taken on a life of its own. It will be read by people you will never meet, and understood in ways that you could not imagine. There will be conversations inspired by your work that would surprise you, baffle you, horrify you and no doubt amuse you. Your words will touch others and change lives, slowly maybe, like water over pebbles, but change will occur nevertheless. Your words may well inspire other writers to take some of your ideas and run with them in quite a different direction. So please keep dragging yourselves from your beds, keep dragging your pens across the page and keep being playful with words.

And for you, dear reader, it's visiting time. Feel free to stroll around the halls, yards, corridors and cells. Peek through the keyhole at lives being lived. Eavesdrop on conversations and private thoughts. But also, be prepared to be taken on wild flights of fancy far beyond these prison walls.

Stewart Ennis is a freelance writer and playwright. His debut novel, Blessed Assurance, *will be published by Vagabond Voices in November 2019. He was lecturer in Creative Writing at HMP Shotts until 2018.*

Visiting Time

The Visit Hall Beckons

the visit hall beckons
familiar faces
conjure up images
of freedom.
one hour of dad's infectious laughter.
the weans are runnin riot,
mair interested in sweets.
mum asks, "how you doin?"
"ah'm fine." ah tell her.
"yer brother came hame drunk", she says
"he'll end up in here wi you."

by Anon

Too much NOISE

Too much **NOISE**
All around
Far too much
Abundant **sound**
Screaming **shouting!!!**
Industrial *banging*
So much **NOISE**
Constant **clanging**
Hissing ringing
In the ears
Too much **NOISE**
Over the years
Cringing jumping
At the slightest **sound**
Nerves *screaming*
With NOISEso **LOUD**
Why do you need to be told?
Quiet **please**
I'm grumpy and old

by Anon

Join the Queue

I queue up for my breakfast
I queue up for my tea
I queue up for my dinner
and it's really bugging me.
I wake up in the morning
and queue up for a shower
and when I get to my canteen
I queue up for an hour.
Each week I queue to change my kit-
it really should be better-
and when the mail is handed out
I queue up to get my letter.
I queue to see the doctor,
I queue to cut my hair;
the only time I never queue
is when there's no queue there.

But I know that when I leave here,
the first thing I will do
is go into the very first shop I see …
… and join another effing queue!

by Anon

Her Majesty's Pleasure

Here I am
at "Her Majesty's Pleasure",
vegetables like snooker balls,
mashed potato
that can hold bricks together
to build a house
they can put
more prisoners into.

by Anon

First Night

I was quite happy with myself. Of course, at this point I was still on my twelve-day Valium detox that most inmates feel obliged to take, to ease the 'settling in' process. They don't just hand the Valium out willy-nilly by the way! Most of my colleagues have to tell a few lies to get their hands on them, but I was nursing ongoing alcoholism and a budding, hard drugs problem at the time. The thing is, when you know it's coming, it's easier to adjust to. And from the age of fifteen, I had known that the day would come when my liberty would have to be suspended. With this frame of mind – and let's not beat around the bush about the extent of carnage I was churning up behind me – I had accepted it long before it came to be. In fact, to most of the people around me, my date with destiny was late.

My *first night* was in * * * Youth Remand Centre. I was twenty-five but every prisoner that came in to the system at that time had to spend a few long days there with the effin monkeys. That would change at a later date when some mum found out that her tender sixteen-year-old son was in with the big bad men. It is a bit of a no-brainer to keep the young upstarts away from older hardened criminals. Thing is, with all the testosterone, and the fact that these kids feel they have to make a name for themselves, (something we all want to do in our chosen field) it's often the older cons that need protecting.

So, the *first night*! Well, let me tell you something about the first night. In the last 24 to 48 hours, you have been picked off the street, or out of your bed – taken to a police station and questioned for anything between 15 minutes and 15 hours – depending on your crime. Then, you lie around the police station and head to court first thing in the morning, where you have your 5 minutes in court and 10 minutes with your lawyer and then – remanded in custody and sent to whatever jail is nearest at the time. Then, you go through the rigmarole of actually getting into the jail, which for the most part is about waiting, filling in forms and telling nurses that you're not suicidal. [At this point, let's not forget the Valium you'll be needing!] So, after all that excitement, by the time the first night comes, a wee bit of TV and a good sleep is on the cards. It's over the next day or two that you can start to get scared and let things get on top of you.

If you don't have enemies on the outside, and stay away from drugs on the inside, then jail is a safe-ish place. So, my first night was okay, and as I said, I watched a wee bit of TV and had a good sleep. I was lucky though, to be in with a hard-core heroin addict. It's funny, but in just about all other aspects of life, a hard-core heroin addict is bad news. But for a first night in prison, he was a Godsend. It's a rule of thumb that he will know most of the other prisoner's scams and all the do's and don'ts, given that his full-time job of feeding his habit will bring him into jail at least once a month, if not more. And in me, a well built 15 stone non-addict, he sees a meal ticket. So, for the first few days, my 'new best pal' takes me out to exercise, introduces me to prisoners and officers, all the while smoking my snout and trying to work out if I'm good for a tap. This mutually beneficial, symbiotic relationship will help me get on my feet, and may even earn himself a wee bag of smack, courtesy of his host crèche. But after a short time, the relationship is damned, as it is in his nature to overstep the mark or steal some snout or some other shit. It's inevitable that even when he is doing good off me, he will cut the nose right off his face.

by Anon

Portrait of a Prison Cell

I am a prison cell. I start off empty and then I get a man or a woman or maybe a boy or a girl. Sometimes they're upset. Others don't really care much. As they settle in, I start to fill up with stuff; family pictures on my walls. Other stuff. They're always talking to themselves. It's funny. And hey, who said that walls have ears? Because they listen alright my friend. Sometimes they have friends come in to see them. Oh, and there is always an officer coming in and out to check up. Sometimes they just need a bit of comfort. At night I hear them cry for their girlfriend or boyfriend. I let my tears fall too.

by Anon

Mushrooms

We have lots of mushrooms in here, all different shapes and sizes. Now the mushroom next door to me isn't too bad. In fact some people say he's a fun guy to be with. But like I said, he's not the only mushroom around here. The place is full of them, all different types. There are poisonous ones. There are the 'I'm better than you' truffles. And, obviously being in here, a lot of these guys have spent far too much time in the dark. Some mushrooms are only too good at spreading their spores with stories latched on. Some are convinced they have magic in their hearts while other mushrooms are just dim white buttons with no shine. About the only thing all these mushrooms have in common is most of them have grown up in shit.

by AD

The Wish

He wishes he hadn't brought him along;
he's brought nothing but bad luck from
the start. He wishes he had put more
planning into it. He wishes *he'd* driven
the car and not half blind Harry. He wishes
he had done the job on his own. He wishes
he had a good lawyer.

by Anon

What if...

What if…
What if I never went to Fife?
What if I grew up around my family?
What if I stuck in at school?
 What if I never went to Fife?
What if I said no to weed?
What if I never smoked heroin?
 What if I never went to Fife?
What if I managed to keep my job?
What if I wasn't abused by my scumbag father?
 What I never went to Fife?
What if…
What if…
What if I decide to get out of prison, go straight, settle?
What if I never went to Fife?
What if I never went to Fife?

by Anon

Blessed by The Sun

Rays of sunlight flow into my cell,
signalling a new day, a hope that everything will be well.
This celestial being which determines the length of my day,
brings life to this world and keeps darkness at bay.

It provides us with warmth, lights up everything around us,
chases away the gloom of night and the things that repel us.
The remnants of the freezing fog shrivel away,
life gains a foothold over the night's tomb, and out we come
    to play.

The life force of the sun washes over us,
nurturing and defining what exists and surrounds us;
fences, grass, secure buildings.
Shadows cast by barred windows fall over all my belongings.

Frantic dreams of last night are chased into oblivion.
I'm brought back into this circle of life and death that we
    live in.
In this crowded life that we find ourselves in,
what is real anymore? What do we place our hopes in?

Shouts of joy and relief follow the cries of new birth,
the deafening silence of our inevitable death; ready to be
    buried in dirt.
In the face of all of this, the sun soldiers on.
It doesn't care for the fragility of the lives that our hopes are
    built upon.

It is a constant symbol in our lives, something to plan events
    around.
The Sun has been around even before the Earth was round.

Rivers flow unhindered, cliffs slowly eroded by the seas.
Our time is counted in years and months, not countless
  centuries.

While we are inconsequential in the scheme of all things,
it's time we acknowledged the sun and the blessings that it
  brings.

by Anon

Locked

Locked
inside my head.
My thoughts are the guards
My dreams punish me,
replaying nightmares,
over and over.
There is no escaping.

by Anon

Times in Time

Through bars I watch the clock.
Time outside has stopped.

Through bars I watch the skies.
Time outside has stopped.

At night my neighbour cries,
for loved ones lost.
At night my neighbour cries
for what he had before.
At night my neighbour cries
for what his life has cost.
At night my neighbour cries
for love that's never more.

Through bars I watch the clock.
Time outside has stopped.

Through bars I watch the skies.
Time outside has stopped.

by Anon

Vampire

While sunshine warms the world outside,
my life is dreary and dead inside.
Boredom is what fate has in store for me,
To be sad, discontented and lonely.
Call me a sceptic, or a complaining old fool.
To you, being a vampire must seem so cool.
But trust me, life's not fair, it's no jamboree.
Living death is just dead boring,
and as painful as can be.

by Anon

The Vicious Circle

Go off the rails
End up in the cells
Apply for bail
Applications fail
     Back to jail
     Howl and wail
     Receive nice mail
Time drags like a snail
Court date a delay-al
On remand you just sail
Until grassed up – betrayal
Jury, "Guilty" they say all

I'm always stressin

But I never learn my lesson

by AD

Walk with a Swagger!

A Ballad

I walked with a swagger, my mouth gave out lip,
On both my broad shoulders sat bloody great chips.
On my arms I laid tracks, no train ever ran down!
And I never concealed them, those tracks were my
crown!

This song I will sing, this tale I will tell
To blinded young lovers, to warn and foretell.
For the rest of my life, in Her Majesty's cell.
It's my personal heaven! It's my personal hell.

I strutted the hall, on fire, fully charged,
I thought 'I'm the main man! I'm living it large!'
But all that went up, came tumbling down,
My charge, it ran out, and I looked like a clown!

This song I will sing, this tale I will tell
To blinded young lovers, to warn and foretell.
For the rest of my life, in Her Majesty's cell.
It's my personal heaven! It's my personal hell.

by N

A View

Sitting, staring at my view
eyes aching for something new,
despairing for nature to show
even a glimpse of an old crow.

by J.R. Duffy

fences

razor wire fences
with snowfall tear drops
the white floor gets deeper

by Anon

Don't Judge Me! Judge Me!

Don't Judge me for what I've done
Judge me as you see me
Don't Judge me because you can
Judge me for what I am
Don't Judge me for the colour of my skin
Judge the person, not the number
Don't judge me from a faraway place
Judge me to my face
Don't judge me because I have faults
Judge me as someone who tries
Don't Judge me before you feel my pain
Judge me fair
        then set me free

by Anon

Got the Jail Head On

Porridge, a breakfast people make in pots
But I'm doing porridge here in SHOTTS

Come to jail, get depressed,
break down and cry.
But I'm smiling every day
as time just rushes by.

Imprisonment is a state of mind,
a wise man once said.
I've still got my freedom.
See it's all in the head.

Some cons moan and moap all day
and then get hooked on drugs.
I see it over and over again.
Some would say they're mugs.

But my drugs are the gym
or going down to education.
A poker addict, I'll play some pool,
lose three hours on the PlayStation.

See now I've got the jail head on
reality goes on hold.
They've got the keys – if we want out on tariff
we best do what we're told.

You might read this wee poem
and think "HE'S F***ING MAD."
But once you're institutionalised
Jail just ain't that bad.

by AD

Come and Get Me

I climb the stairs like a ninja, trying to convince myself that I'm a fearless female fighting machine. I'm holding the automatic in both hands, safety off, just like dad showed me when he took me hunting. I take a deep breath and keeping the gun in front, slowly turn the handle of what looks to be the bathroom door. No matter how many times I've done this it still sends a terrible chill down into my stomach. It's not the bathroom.

On a king size bed are the skeletal remains of a couple. They have done what many have chosen to do, when they have had enough. There is gun in the man's hand. It's not easy, but I manage to take it from him and put it in my backpack. There's a walk-in wardrobe full of women's clothes, all neatly folded, hung and colour coordinated. I consider a skirt or a dress but eventually choose a top and jeans that are near my size.

I go through the same procedure with the other doors. One leads into a cupboard, where I find a few tins of peaches stashed in a drawer. Result, I say to myself. I talk to myself constantly now. It feels natural. I even answer my own questions. I check the other drawers and find one more treasure, a bottle of Valium, prescribed to Mrs G. Shepherd. There are about two dozen tablets. I put them in my pocket. These days they could come in very handy. I find the bathroom and I cannot believe my eyes, a bathtub. Please, please, please, I say to myself, let the hot water be working. Yes! After months living and plundering empty and abandoned houses, I have finally found one with running hot water. I'm dirty beyond belief but that's the norm now. I've not had a wash for over four months. No need, since the world went to shit.

In the corner of the room there is a towel rack with towels folded neatly in the middle rack. The bath is covered in dust so I rinse it out with some water but the glugging from the taps is so loud. What am I doing? My day has gone well so far, too well. I quickly turn off the taps and listen. Nothing.

As the bath fills up, I take my knife and cut a small square from one of the towels to use as a cloth, just big enough to cover my face. Soon the bath is full to the brim with hot water and steam is building up on the window. Like home. I rub some dirt off the window and look out at what's left of the world I used to know and love. Cars are abandoned everywhere, turned over and burnt out. I throw my old clothes in the corner. I won't be wearing them again. I turn off the water and admire the sight of a hot bath, something I'd not have given a second thought to in my old life. I remembered the apple-scented shower gel that I keep in my backpack, a reminder of my baby sister.

I ease myself slowly into the welcoming clean, clear hot water. It immediately turns cloudy from the dirt. I lather myself in the apple shower gel, take a deep breath, and slide under the water. I'm immediately transported back to the south of France and that holiday, playing with my baby sister, while mum and dad sunbathed on the porch.

When I surface, I feel a hunger pang and open one of the tins of peaches, eating them in the bath, and thinking yet again, of how this whole mess started.

Me and my little sister were sitting in the living room. I was helping her with her homework. That's when we heard the newsflash. It was on every network. Something about a laboratory and a virus, so they told us, though I've since heard that was a lie. Whatever it was, it turned people into savage monsters, who bit and ate each other. Dad took us all up to the hunting cabin, well away from the biters, where he taught us to survive. Eventually the food ran out and we looked for a new place. That's when we found that even the people who'd survived had turned nasty.

I dip the cut-out cloth in the water, place it over my face and relax. Relax. Something I used to take for granted. With a belly full of peaches and a bath full of hot water I soon begin to doze off, and dream what is now a common dream.

I'm back at the old farmhouse on the last day I'd ever spend with my family. We'd been there a while, even planted vegetables. Life was … okay. Until we were moved along by people with more guns and more muscle than us. That was the moment I completely lost faith in humanity. We found shelter in an old caravan a few miles from the farm. And then the biters came.

Dad managed to get me safely into the car, but when he went back to the caravan for my mum and sister the biters surrounded them. Dad let off the last his ammo in his sidearm. There was screaming. And then there was silence. I sped off as the biters started to surround me.

There are days I go without eating. Days when I'm tired of it all. Tired of being alone. Tired of having no one to trust. Tired of this world. I start to cry, but immediately stop when I hear the loud banging coming from downstairs. Biters.

I'm not scared. Not anymore. I'm all scared out. I reach over for the bottle of tablets and another tin of peaches, pour the contents of the bottle into my mouth and wash them down with peach juice

There's a crash. Soon they'll be inside and climbing the stair. Soon I'll hear that constant death rattle that is the sound of biters' breathing.

I lie down in the hot water as the medication takes hold. I'm smiling. I feel like mum when she drank too much at Christmas. Somewhere there is banging on the bathroom door. But I'm well away. In a daydream. With my family. In those happiest of moments.

by R.J. Duffy

Fitzy's Fear of Education

Scene One

Joe, 20s, is in his cell, watching crap telly, laid back. Fitzy,20s, enters, pacing up & down, talking twenty to the dozen.

Fitzy: Awright Joe? How ye daen bro? Settlin in? That's a week noo eh? Since the transfer.

Joe: (*Doesn't lift his eyes from the telly*) Brand new mucker. Conditions are a lot better than that last shit hole, eh Fitzy boy.

Fitzy: (*More anxious*) Here Joe, Joe. Whit ye gonnae pick fur education mate? Dae ye just pick any auld shite? Eh? Ah mean ye don't need tae dae tests or anythin dae ye bro?

Joe: (*Fed up with questions*) How dae ah know? It's ma first time in a jail that does aw this education pish. Ah know wan thing but! They cannae teach this auld dog fuck all!

Scene Two

Joe and Fitzy are hanging about in the foyer of the Education Centre. Joe is relaxed, reading a paper. Fitzy again is pacing up & down, even more nervous, biting his nails, Joe tries to ignore it but it's too much.

Joe: Fitzy ye awright mate? Yer acting a bit weird.

Fitzy looks around to make sure no-one else is listening.

Fitzy: Joe, listen mate. Ye know ah'm a bit of a boy. Well

respected. A bit of a face shall we say eh? Whit ah'm aboot tae tell ye...ye better no say a word tae naebdy. Ah mean it Joe.

Joe: C'moan Fitzy. Ah thought ye knew me by noo. Ah'm solid. Whit ye tell me stays between you n me bro. Promise ye.

Fitzy: (*This isn't easy for him*) Thing is Joe... ah...ah cannae ...ah cannae read or write at aw.

Joe: Ah thought you went tae school?

Fitzy: Aye but ah did fuck aw at school. Ah wis always gettin kicked oot for bein a clown and fightin wi emdy n everybody mate.

Joe: Here Fitzy, tell ye whit, ah cannae hardly read or write either. Just ma name. Even that's a struggle. Let's keep it tae oorsels. We don't want folk thinkin we're a couple a eejits eh?

Scene Three

Linda, the teacher is already in the classroom. Joe, looking cocky sits down. The nervous Fitzy sits beside him. Linda is sorting through some papers. Fitzy waits nervously for Linda to speak.

Linda: Hi. I'm Linda. Welcome to the induction to education. Anything you'd like to ask?

Joe: Naw.

Fitzy: (*Hides his nervousness with cockiness*) Nae danger hen. You carry oan.

Linda: Okay. I've two sets of papers for you to complete, on basic English and Maths. Nothing too hard. You boys take your time. I'll mark them up when you're done

Joe: (*He leans over, quietly*) Aw naw ! Noo whit?

Fitzy: "Aw naw" nuffin. At least you can write a wee bit. Ah've no goat a scooby. So ur we gonnae embarrass oorsels and tell her …or whit?

Joe: Are we fuck. We're no sayin a word tae naebdy. We agreed. Let's get oot a here.

Fitzy: (*Not convinced*) Ah'm cool wae that bro. Who needs education in jail anyway eh?

Joe and Fitzy get up and head for the door, without any explanation.

Linda: Have you finished already?

Joe: Naw Linda doll. Education's no fur these boys.

Fitz stops, like he's about to say something to Linda

Joe: Ur ye comin Fitzy?

Fitzy: (*Unsure*) Eh…whit?…eh…aye… right…ah'm at yer back mucker.

Linda: (*Hands him a pink form*) Take this. If you change your mind you can always come back.

Fitzy: Cheers missus.

Joe: (*Reappears*) Aye good try doll …but Naw…we'll no be comin' back, eh Fitzy?

They leave, Fitzy doesn't know what to do with the leaflet so shoves it in his back pocket.

Scene Four

Joe's cell. Joe is watching crap telly, chilled out. Fitzy stands at the door but doesn't go inside.

Fitzy: Eh... Joe.

Joe: (*Eyes on telly*) Whit?

Fitzy: Dae ye think that wis a good move back there?

Joe: (*Still watching telly*) Whit dae ye mean?

Fitzy: Well ...thing is...we're baith daen long sentences eh?

Joe: (*Still watching telly*) Aye...and ah don't need remindin.

Fitzy: Should we no ...mebbe ...use it tae oor advantage?

Joe: (*Stares at him*) Advantage? Whit advantages ur here tae daen a lang sentence?

Fitzy: We could mebbe use the time tae learn tae read n write...ye know ... better oorselves. Mebbe even get a few qualifications behind us.

Joe: (*Laughs*) Fuck off Fitzy. Ah'm no embarrassin masel in front a naebody.

Fitzy: But...

Joe: 'But' nothing... that's the end of it. Are ye coming in or whit? Smoke n a coffee ? Ma treat? (*He turns his attention back to the telly*)

Fitzy: (*About to go in, but hesitates & takes the pink education form from his back pocket*)) Tell ye whit…ah'll come back in a bit. There's something ah need tae dae first.

The End

by Anon

Liberation Blues

It's getting close to liberation
Man I just can't wait
It's getting so close to my liberation
Oh man I cannot wait
I need to make damn sure on my release
That I keep a real clean slate

I'll need to make some new friends
Cos ma old friends I don't rate,
Yeah, I'm gonna make some new friends
Cos those old friends I just don't rate
All those years I was in prison
They never booked one visit at the gate

It's getting close to liberation
Man I just can't wait
It's getting so close to my liberation
Oh man I cannot wait
I need to make damn sure on my release
That I keep a real clean slate

Don't wanna hear those so-called friends' excuses
It's way too late
No I don't hear those lame excuses
It's way way too late
I don't wanna be around them anyway
Cos they aint nothing but jail bait

> *It's getting close to liberation*
> *Man I just can't wait*
> *It's getting so close to my liberation*
> *Oh man I cannot wait*

I need to make damn sure on my release
That I keep a real clean slate

by Anon

Schadenfreude

The solace
of my silent, serene cell,
is broken,
by the resonating screech of the prison panic alarm.
Officers switch to busy beaver mode,
scrambling in reverse gear,
to attend this terrifying, uncertain scene;
perhaps a fight,
maybe an escape attempt;
disrespect being aimed
at vulnerable hardened souls,
drugs coming over the fence,
a mobile phone.

Challenging the silence,
a squadron of busy worker bees,
all so gently mannered;
After you!
No, after you!
The tranquil finds its way back to the hall.
Much heightened chitter chatter,
along with speculative theories
on that evening's dramatics.

Elevated enjoyment rings out,
because if I am here, then
I was not
involved.

by Anon

Dark Place

(Inspired by a prison friendship)

My dear friend,
We've stood together so many years, sharing our hopes and fears. You've always been so strong, and the advice you gave me will stay with me. But recently you've been hiding away, sometimes for days. It seems that time has taken its toll on you. Your appearance has become dishevelled. I've seen the blank stare. I fear you're leaving us, for a dark and lonely place. In your head, your friends have become your enemies. You shun the help they offer. Demons and devils have taken over, filling your peaceful thoughts with whispers. I've never felt as helpless as you push me aside and head off into this deep dark place. My friend, I will never stop trying to make you see the light.

by EM

The Ramblings of a Grumpy Old Man

A Rant

Morning comes again. Time to take the *tartan tablets*. Don't know if it's getting harder or easier. Memory's going, slowly. Fell over yesterday. Dropped the kettle as well. My shaking hands. They just seem to forget how to hold on to things. Keep getting confused. Disoriented. Don't know if I'm coming or going at times. It all makes life more difficult by the day.

I look at Joey. Or auld Peter. They're worse than me. And only a couple of years older. Sixty this year. I think. Can't remember even the basic things at times. Have to write it down on a scrap of paper. Then I lose the paper. It's somewhere in my cell. I think.

Ah, the trials of old age. Dementia. Parkinson's. Strokes. Cancer. Heart disease. But in here there's no proper care. Not til the last few weeks of life. The rules don't take us old lags into consideration. We're just have to struggle on. Try to keep up. Some of the young prisoners are decent enough. But most of them are wrapped up in drugs. They can be boisterous. It's expected; the protocol needed for survival behind bars. That can be scary to us old boys. Then there's the noise. Like trying to sleep in a disco. Thank God I'm nearly deaf.

No, prisons are not set up for us auld yins. And there's more of us each year. Day's not far off when the undertaker will be a constant visitor. Carting off the dead from age related illness. No one seems to care.

Why can't they have halls that cater for problems with old age? Why can't they train young pass men in palliative care and first aid? Why can't they have cells with rails and seats in the showers? Why can't they allow us more time to answer questions, to deal with problems. Even simple things like visiting the doctor or collecting our meals. It wouldn't take much. To go at a slower pace. Aye, chance will be a fine thing.

Just hope I'm dead before I get to the stage where I'm having to lie in a pish and shit soaked bed. Before I'm the hall joke.

Maybe one day. When prisons are overcrowded with sick old men. Maybe then. But how many will have to go through illness and humiliation? How many will suffer the terror and threats of violence we now face behind bars? Us, the frustrated grumpy old men.

by Anon

Going Out On a High

Some Thoughts on a Prison Performance Project

I participated in the devised theatre week organized by the *Royal Scottish Conservatoire* Contemporary Performance Department. I'd heard about it in the creative writing class that I attend weekly. I've spent many years in and out of prison and to be perfectly honest I've never opted to get involved in anything remotely similar. Why then did I get involved in this?

I can't give you anything better than it was *something different* – and I was persuaded by my creative writing teacher. I can't say I gave it enough thought to have any fears. I really didn't imagine *anything*. I came as an open book. And I'm really glad I did. I got more out of it than I would have doing the other things I do every week. I really enjoyed the performance day. I had a ball and the feedback I got from it was very very positive. Having spent most of my life abusing substances, my confidence is very low. It's part of the lie of addiction. Therefore speaking publicly is something I avoid religiously. I stretched my inner self whilst nervous. I coped!

I arrived on the Monday, not really knowing what to expect, but enthusiastic. I had some ideas of my own but the teachers led us in a particular direction away from my ideas which I never did get to share. On reflection though, I realise that my ideas would have been impossible to produce within the time frame.

I did start to get a little dejected on the Wednesday. I just couldn't see how we could possibly manage to produce a performance by the Friday. I think it's notable that the single person, who started but didn't complete the course and perform, left after this day. Although, to be fair, the performance time was changed and subsequently his family couldn't come at the new time.

Thursday was a breath of fresh air. Everything was shaped

and put together. It appeared we had something that could actually be called 'a show'!

Friday was performance day. The audience was made up of families, prison staff,one or two from STIR, the prison Magazine, and theatre students. It was ample. As I said earlier, self-esteem and confidence are a bit of a problem for me. Perhaps events such as these are something to look at in conquering that part of my recovery. Most doctors will tell you that for such a problem the best thing you can do is go to the gym, but what if you're not very sporty?

All the performers were given a chance to shine and recharge their batteries, but I enjoy music and my favourite part of the whole performance was Eddie's song, *The Games People Play*, right at the end of the show. We all stood on chairs, clapping and singing along to the anthem-like chorus.

> *La-da da da da da da da*
> *La-da da da da da da dee*
> *Talking 'bout you and me*
> *And the games people play*

Tony was good on guitar and Eddie sang it brilliantly. It was a fitting way to end the show – on a high!

The whole thing seemed to be well received by the audience. There were many laughs – during and after – and everyone I spoke to thought it was really good. I'm certain that they were telling me the truth. After so many years in prison, you become an expert in body language, constantly looking for what people are not telling you.

by BK

Games People Play by Joe South
Lyrics © Sony/ATV Music Publishing LLC, The Bicycle Music Company

Six Wishes

He wishes things could be more peaceful.
He wishes he had never done it.
He wishes he was going home to his family.
He wishes he had stayed at school.
He wishes he had listened to his mother.
He wishes he could turn back time.

by Anon

The Caged Rat

(After Maya Angelou's The Caged Bird)

The caged rat longs for the bowels of a ship
The free rat is cunning and lives by its wits
The caged rat is pulled at and prodded and poked
The free rat is vicious, his bite is no joke
The caged rat craves the company of its clan
The free rat has never known the cruel hand of man
The caged rat is lonely, no friends can it find
The free rat is social and it knows its own mind
The caged rat lives in constant fear
The free rat feasts on crumbs and spilt beer
The caged rat knows only steel and straw
But the free rat,
the free rat,
has conquered the world.

by DG

A Memorable Journey

When my heart sinks and fills with dreaded fears,
I seek comfort in urgent whispers of prayers, now filling my ears.
I lift my head; look at dark skies through my hands,
stare at clouds drifting away to faraway lands,
bearing gifts of rain, a type of succour,
washing away sorrows in whatever shape they occur.

Birds live in trees that line the long road ahead,
Singing songs of hope and of good lives they've led.
They lift my spirit and give me a strange longing,
of straight pathed lives, of not coveting other's belongings.
I wish I could smile and stop all this useless whinging,
but after all these years imprisoned, do you expect me to be singing?

Memorable journeys are made to fulfil plans that we make,
of dreams, of good times; of sacrifices made for our sake.
The question of my existence pierces my heart on dark nights.
It pains me to exist, does God have me in his sights?
I had a dream, a vision of the journeys I'd undertake,
but now I'm locked up in here, my life is at stake.

Pray for me, while I try to understand the life I've led.
I think of it daily while lying in bed.
I would love to sail oceans, explore dark forests,
but pondering my life is now my personal Everest.

Sunshine pours into my cell, but there's only darkness inside.
These journeys mean nothing to those of you outside.
Journeys in prison; filled with sorrow,
as memorable today as they will be tomorrow.

by Anon

The Auld Weegie Blues

There was a wee man fae Glesga
who spent his hale life in jail.
He was a right wee character
though he was auld and frail,
Aw day lang he tellt his jokes
aw aboot his life o' sin,
how the polis ayeweys nicked him when he got oot
and sent him straight back in.

Though he never killed a man
a life sentence he has done,
for every crime he committed
he got caught for every one.
As he shuffles up and doon the hall
wi his shoogly Zimmer frame
he tells his jokes and makes ye laugh
even though he is in pain.

He disnae want tae harm you
or gie you an awfy fright;
he only wants tae have some fun
each and every night.
So if ye hear that click click clickin
stoppin by yer door,
ask him in tae tell a joke,
ye'll be laughin til yer sore.

Noo he is nae longer
he died a lonely death,
spent his life in prison
right up tae his final breath.
But at night ye can still hear him
shufflin alang that hall
and ye can hear his Glesga laughter
echoin aff the prison walls.

by Anon

ahv made it

ah used tay kick a baw affa wa
which ah thoat wiz braw.
        dreamz ah playin in the hoops
        n aw that.
ah used tay play tennis oan the road
which is a snobby game wher ahm fay
        dreamz ah wimbledon
        n aw that
ah used tay jump ramps oan bmx's
jumpin ower lined up pals
        dreamz ah wiz evel kneavel
        n aw that
ah used tay run roon the block
an in in the park
        dreamz ah the olympics
        n aw that
ah'll day aw these whin ahm aulder
ahd say tay masel

n ah did

ah made it
ah play fitba
ah play tennis
ah even ride bikes
n ah run

but HMP Shotts
hiznay goat
its ain Olympic team

                                    by T

Back To The Future

Back to the wall, emotions will start
To flood through your heart and mind;
The adrenalin will make you shake. The
Future will start when this is over.

by Anon

Christmas Visit

Gloom
gone,
presents, tinsel,
grumpy screws cracking smiles
kids excited
emotional cons,
"Time up! Say your goodbyes!"
Back to normality's grey mundane.

Always
tough
this time of year

by Anon

Inside Out

I was led off the bus, handcuffed to the security officer, and entered the reception doors. That was when I was felt overcome with fear. My hands were trembling and sweat was pouring down my forehead. Then I was searched and told which cell block I'd be living in.

The stench of grease and sweat, and the faceless voices shouting or roaring with laughter, was overpowering. The officer banged the gate closed behind me and locked it. Silence. One hundred and thirty burning eyes stared at me like I was an alien. I was led up the stairs and along the landing, the other prisoners whispering as we walked.

"Stop there!" said an officer. I entered the cell that was to be my home, turned round and …

SLAM! The door was locked. My time had begun.

Getting used to prison life was hard. I was depressed and lonely. I missed my family. I'd see them once a week for one hour, but what is that when you're used to them being a part of your everyday life? Everything I'd taken for granted came rushing to the surface. Especially my daughter. I was full of regrets for all those times I'd made excuses to get out of spending the weekend with her so I could go out drinking with mates. I realized just how selfish I'd been.

Things get easier with time and I made a few *jail buddies*. We'd sit together and smoke, drink coffee, play cards and tell each other our stories. I began to go to education, filling my whole week up with classes. I'd left school with no qualifications whatsoever, so I jumped at this chance to try again. I started to feel happy again. I'd wake up excited about the day ahead rather than dreading it. I also realized something important about myself; I was a lot more intelligent that I believed. I was determined to keep my head down and try to gain something I could use after my release.

After a couple of months, I almost felt that I wasn't in prison anymore. Day by day, week by week, month by month I would spend as many hours as I could, completing courses and passing exams. Almost every week I sent home a new certificate and each time my family would tell me how proud they were. With every certificate, every positive comment, my confidence and self-esteem grew and grew.

Slowly but surely, time slipped by and my release date got closer. My mother had been sending me photographs of my daughter; on day outs with her Grandma and Granddad, having fun at Halloween, opening presents on Christmas morning or playing with her cousins. Some nights I lay on my bed for hours, just staring at them. I'd missed it all. I had five favourite pictures of her. Her first day in Primary 1. Her first day in Primary 2 and her first days in Primary 3, 4 and 5. I placed them in a row. I couldn't believe how much she'd had changed over the course of four years. I hadn't noticed because I was only seeing her one hour a week. I was getting her school reports sent in and there was nothing but positive comments. Her teachers wrote of her being top of her class in all subjects, and how polite and well-mannered she was. I was so proud of her.

But none of her achievements had anything to do with my role as a father. I couldn't take credit for any of it, and so I promised myself, there and then I would never let her down again.

I was coming towards the end of my sentence. My daughter was constantly, gleefully, reminding me on the phone and at visits how long I had left.

"Seven days left daddy! ... Two days left daddy!"

My second last night, I hardly slept. My *gate fever* was at a whole new level. I thought I was going to burst. One day to go. and I could already feel the sun on my skin, and the wind in my hair.

At last an officer called my name, and I looked down over the balcony,

"That's you," he said, "gather your stuff."

Liberation!

I said goodbye to the boys in the hall before I was taken to reception. After being searched for one last time and signing the paperwork, I was led to the gate.

My daughter ran towards me, bursting with excitement, "Yay Daddy," she shouted, "you're coming home!"

"I know princess," I said, kneeling down and grabbing her. "And I promise that I'll never leave you again. This is it. I'm out for good".

by Anon

Ah Cannae Write A Poem Tae Order

Write a poem!
I was ordered tae do.
Nae chance ah thought;
ah'll lea' that shit tae you

Don't give me,
it's not your 'kind of thing'
Close your eyes, open your mind,
see what images your thoughts may bring

Ah've no got ma glesses
Ah'm as blin as a bat
Nae pencil, nae rubber
Ah've no got any a that

Aw ah see
is the picture in front a me;
a lang windin road disappearin intae thin air,
fu' a sheep, grass n dykes.
Stuff that!
Ah'm no gawn there.

It looks as boring as this stupit class
Clever teacher talkin' oot his arse
Its easy fur him wi his education.
Ah'll jist stick tae ma prescribed medication.

Ah'm a busy man.
Ah've no got time
tae sit here dain' the impossible,
n comin' up wi some nonsensical rhyme.

The idea is absurd.
And that's ma final word!

by Anon

ahm bad

the judge sez "yer bad"
ah sez "ahm no"

the judge sez "yer bad"
ah sez "ahm no!"

the judge sez "yer bad"
ah sez "ahm no!"

the judge fuckin won

Someone to make the black blue

all I want
is someone to tear limb from limb,
someone to whisper in my ear
all I want is the here and now,
someone to play the strings of my heart,
someone to break the monotony
all I want
is someone to walk the journey
someone to sometimes carry me
all I want
is someone to make the black, blue
all I want is you

by DG

Stand Up and Be Counted

I'm flavoured by jail sauce
Don't have any gold to floss
Calling a person I don't know, Boss
Feeling crucified to the cross

So kick me, beat me, you'll never defeat me.

Here I go, I've found my flow
Sit back, watch me go
Mad man with a mad plan
See life so freely aint no scam

So kick me, beat me, you'll never defeat me.

Got my mind thinking
Subliminal thoughts shaking
The good in me's winning
The nutter is losing

So kick me, beat me, you'll never defeat me.

I'm the maker of my own downfall
I drove and crashed into a wall
I got back up and I stood tall
I accepted it's all my fault

So kicking me and beating me
did defeat me,
til I admitted the lot
and hit the rock.
There was no saving me
til one day I saw it so clearly

Don't kick me – or beat me – don't defeat me.

Present moment, in my gaff, I own it
All the bad I've done no longer fits it
I'm a man who's went through it all
To my victims, I'm sorry, I was mental

Took thirty four years to be shook
Reading loads of books
The curse of pain is the route
To learning about an inner truth

Don't kick me – or beat me – don't defeat me
Coz at long last,
I'm ready.

by Anon

I Want To tell You

I want to tell you not to worry,
that nobody in here gets out in a hurry.
I want to tell you
that even though I'm doing time,
that even though I'm on my own,
I'm not alone.
I want to tell you
that each and every day
you're by my side.

by Anon

A Class Act

Act One

Two prisoners are sitting eating their dinner in the hall.

Tonk: Education? Whit good wid gawn back tae school be? Ah mean ah'm nae spring chicken. Naebody's gawni gie me a joab just coz ah've goat a bit a paper wi a couple o' ticks oanit.

Vitz: It's no like that. It gets ye oot the hall and away fae the usual shite that ye huv tae pit up wi every day.

Tonk: Gie us a brek. If ah wiz that clever ah widnae huv ended up in here

Vitz: Naw, gie *yersel* a brek n gie it a go! Whit herm wid it dae?

Act Two

Tonk enters a basic English literacy class. He is the only one there, apart from the tutor, Julie.

Julie: Well, it looks like it's just the two of us. I'm Julie. Tell me, what are you expecting from the class, and what would you like to achieve?

Tonk: Well, ah huvnae really thoat aboot it. Ah suppose ah jist want tae improve ma writin.

Julie: *Can* you write?

Tonk: Aye! Ah'm no fuckin stupit ye know!

Julie: I didn't say you were. Tell you what, you show me a little respect, by watching your language, and I'll show you all the respect you want by helping you improve your use of language. Deal

Tonk: Deal. Sorry aboot that. Ah've jist goat so used tae bein oan the defensive.

Julie: I'm not here to put you down. I've no doubt there are plenty of others who do, but not me. Okay, let's see. Write down five words. Any words that come into your head, and I'll do the same.

Tonk and Julie write down their five words

Tonk: Right, done. But they don't make any sense.

Julie: Okay. Here are my five words; *music, perfume, hungry, bicycle* and *juggling*. What are yours?

Tonk: *Football, the boozer, television, daughter* n *crisps*.

Julie: Now we'll swap our lists. I want you to take my words back to your cell and write a short story, about a hundred words, which must include my five words. I'll take yours and do the same thing at home and we'll share our stories next week. How does that sound?

Tonk: A *hunner words*? Ah don't even ken a hunner words. But ah'll gie it a go as long as you dae it an aw.

Act Three

Six months later. Julie's classroom. There are six students there now. Tonk rushes in, excitedly waving a letter!
Tonk: (*Shouting*) Julie! Julie! Ah jist goat this letter this

mornin! It says ah've won a writin competition! Dae ye know anythin' aboot it?

Julie: (*She takes the letter from Tonk*) Wow! This is brilliant. (…) Do you remember that very first day you came into my class, and I asked you to go away and write a short story?

Tonk: Aye.

Julie: Well, I was so impressed with it, I sent it away for you. Remember I asked you if it was alright to do so?

Tonk: Aye, but ah thought ye were jokin!

Julie: No Tonk. Your writing had honesty and integrity. It was your story. No one else could have written it. That is why the judges have picked up on it.

Tonk: Ah cannae believe that there are people oot there that would describe me as honest! It is a nice thought though. It jist goes tae show ye, education is mair than a wee bit a paper.

Curtain closes to thunderous applause.

by Anon

Empty Page

My head is empty.

So's this page.

The rest of the class are

throwing out sonnets,

tapping their pencils.

I'm jealous with rage.

This set rhyming scheme caper

aint my bonnet.

by GB

Poor Blind Mice

Poor blind mice, poor blind mice
All got high to have some fun
Carried a knife, carried a gun
All got addicted one by one
Poor blind mice, poor blind mice.

Poor blind mice, poor blind mice
Used the knife carried the gun
Killed a man went on the run
Life of crime is no much fun
Poor blind mice, poor blind mice

Poor bind mice, poor blind mice
Used the knife, took a life
Lost their friends, family and wife
Sent to prison for the rest of their lives
Poor blind mice, poor blind mice

Poor blind mice poor blind mice
One by one they walk the hall
Caged like animals see them crawl
Enjoyed being high, now feeling small
Poor blind mice, poor blind mice

by Anon

Ah Don't Take Visits Any Mair

Ah don't take visits any mair
Ahm oot eh here soon
So ah'll see the bastarts
moanin faces soon enough.

Sittin ther listenin tae,
"Everybody's daein great!"
An aw ahm hinkin is,
Hope ther gonnae pit PPC oan fur me.*
Ur
"Aw ah forgot tae get chynge
 fur the vendin machine."
An ahm hinkin
That's me fuckt fur a bar a choacolate.

Nah,
ah don't take visits any mair

by Anon

---

*   *PPC*: Prisoner's Personal Cash (between £5 and £20 a week

The Art of Fly Tying

Hook clamped in place,
bobbin at the ready,
tinsel and thread,
a hand so steady.

Finest of fibres;
tail of mink,
body of hare,
a ribbed golden tint.

A grizzle cock finish,
this fly won't sink.
Tumbling with the breeze,
comes the *Grizzle Mink*.

by Anon

A Vision of Clementines

I was asked, *What reminds you of Christmas?*
I sat and pondered
and eventually a smile spread across my face,
as memories of people and times,
of songs and games we played,
of smiles filling the room
or laughter exploding at some family joke.

And a vision of Clementines
sat in a small wooden box
bright orange
with little leaves of green.

Christmas cards pinned to my Nan's door,
fighting with the kids as they push me out of bed
at some crazy hour, so they can open their gifts.
That silence that came after everyone was fed.
Sitting and watching *Star-Wars* with my dad in eighty five
 and again twenty years on with my own kids.

And a vision of Clementines
sat in their small wooden box
bright orange
with little leaves of green

by Anon

empty chair

light blue sky, warmth of sun
cold beer, the clink of ice in mum's spiced rum
barbeque smoke mixing with skunk
tapping of feet to *Fools Gold Funk*
children laugh, splashing without a care
daisies and bluebells in their hair

but no-one mentions that empty chair

by GB

Andy

A Scot and a Serb,
not a bad joke, but
history being made.

A country united at the edge of their seats,
square eyes;
gasps fill homes and pubs,
drinks go undrunk.

Is this the final serve?

Simultaneously millions rise to their feet
(an earthquake of pride)
as one Scot falls to his knees:

relieved.

by CR

If I was not such a Solemn Dude

If I was not such a solemn dude
I'd raise my spirits if I could,
and chase my upside-down smile.
People would stop running a mile,
if I was not such a solemn dude,
if I was not such a solemn dude.

by Anon

Ju Jitsu

There was wee man frae Crewe
On tip-toe he stood two fit two
Don't make fun o' his size
This wouldnae be wise,
This wee man he knows ju- jitsu

by Anon

Bad Judgement

As an inexplicable mid-autumn sun dazzled the east end of Glasgow, bathing everything in shining gold as though Midas himself had run a hand over it, Ashleigh Mickelson trundled up Alexandra Parade, the golden rays turning her blond hair as yellow as a daffodil.

Ashleigh had trained as a Social Worker in Chelsea, but had recently moved to *The Child and Family* department in Parkhead, Glasgow. Despite its challenges, Ashleigh thought the world of her job, and harboured aspirations of running her own team.

As she caught sight of her reflection in an estate agency window. *I need to lose weight.* Ashleigh was not seriously overweight, and yet here she was on her way to the pharmacists to find out about slimming programmes.

As Ashleigh stood in the queue to speak to the pharmacist, she scanned the shelves like a sniper searching for a target. She spotted an elegant woman, in expensive greys, speaking into a mobile phone that was decorated with a red and yellow butterfly. It was identical to her own. When Ashleigh saw that the woman was clutching a black *Prada* handbag, she felt her stomach tighten, but put it off as hunger. She rummaged around for her purse in her own bag, acutely aware now of how cheap it looked compared to the woman's and realised with utter dismay that her own mobile phone was missing. She checked and double checked her pockets, her eyes darted side-to-side, searching the floor in case it'd fallen out, and finally coming to rest upon the elegant woman with her identical device. She gently tapped the lady in grey on the shoulder,

"Excuse me."

The woman turned, frowning,

"Can I help you?" she said, curtly.

Ashleigh flushed,

"I don't wish to be rude …" she began.

'Well, don't!' the lady in grey snapped, "I'm on the phone."

Ashleigh realised it was highly unlikely that a woman such as this, could have taken her phone, but she had to be certain, and steeling herself for another scolding as if she was a petulant child, Ashleigh tapped the woman on the shoulder once more, a little more firmly this time,

"Excuse me, but…"

The woman spun round,

"For the love of…".

"I'm sorry!" said, Ashleigh, attempting an air of authority, "But I believe you may have my phone.'

The woman hissed with barely contained rage, enunciating each word

"I-beg-your-pardon!"

The lady-in-grey's anger and her cherry-red face unnerved Ashleigh, making her stomach twist and turn like a rollercoaster, but her will remained strong.

"I said," repeated Ashleigh, hands balled into fists now, "I believe you may have my phone." Her voice came out a little more sharply than she intended as she struggled to contain her own anger, but it had the desired effect; the lady in grey recoiled as if she had been slapped.

"I…what…" The woman shook herself back into something approximating composure, "I have no idea what you're talking about! This is *my* phone! I am absolutely appalled by your accusation!'

Before she could stop herself, Ashleigh had pounced on the woman like a lion attacking a gazelle, grabbing at the red and yellow butterfly phone. The women now raked at each other, their painted nails scratching the other's face, neck, anything that they could get to, all the while, shrieking at the tops of their voices.

During the commotion, the familiar sound of a siren pierced the mayhem like a knife through glass. Ashleigh froze and as she did so, took a fist to the face that caused a starburst of lights to explode behind her eyelids as if someone had let off a firework inside her head. She immediately fell into unconsciousness.

Later, Ashleigh would come to reflect how her lapse in judgement would cause the problems she'd only ever heard about, from her colleagues in the Criminal Justice department.

FIN

by S

But I'm Not Tired

Suede fronds of grass
Under running fingers
Screaming freckled mass
Like sunlight, lingers

Sun cooked filthy faces
Green skint knees
Wooded play army bases
Full o' jealous bees

Bucket filled Hippo dipping
Splash paddle pool
Wrinkled folk hedge clipping
Icer queue drool

Grilled pitch toffee tar
Lucky feet avoid
Black sky from afar
Lightning show enjoyed

Weeks lived in days
Without any clocks
Fed on golden rays
Each day unlocks

by GK

Love in the Pouring Rain

I met a girl one cold grey night
When I was waiting for the Paisley train
That's right, I met a girl one cold grey night
When I was waiting for the Paisley train
We were sitting in the shelter
Keeping out of the pouring rain

She said, *Can I have a cigarette?*
And then she asked ma name
She said, *Heh, can I have a cigarette?*
Then she asked ma name
So I whispered it in her ear then said,
I cannot be tamed.

Chorus
I been missin you baby
I've been missin you so bad
I been missin you girl
I've been missin you so bad
I can't sleep at night
I miss the fun we had

She said, *Where you headed?*
I said, *The Big City, out west*
She said, *Tell, me where you headed?*
I said, *The Big City – way out west*
She said, *Do you mind if I follow?*
Well… you can imagine the rest.

I been missin you baby
I've been missin you so bad
I been missin you girl
I've been missin you so bad
I can't sleep at night
I miss the fun we had

by Anon

Fly when they want you to fall

A song

Chorus: Don't be scared by the poison
Cause there's always a reason
Search out the truth in it all
Fly when they want you to fall

The people tonight they don't want to eat
There's feasts a plenty at their feet
Those souls we see they're not alive
Slaves of a culture nine to five

Empty dreams and no ambition
Go tell God he's failed his mission
System's all set up to break you down
You sweat all day to pay the crown

Chorus: Don't be scared by the poison
Cause there's always a reason
Search out the truth in it all
Fly when they want you to fall

Try your best to stand out from the crowd
If you understand, shout it out loud
People in your street are your family
Once we're all together just wait and see

Soon the situation will be new
You will look at me and I'll look at you
Everyone is happy but can it last
We want to leave the past in the past.

Chorus: Don't be scared by the poison
Cause there's always a reason
Search out the truth in it all
Fly when they want you to fall

By AD

Ma Wee Maw

She's a navvy workin' doon a hole
She's the twenty pack a' *Consulate Menthol*
She's the *Johnny Walker* blended whisky
She's the china tea set n the green tea cosy
She's *My Yiddish Mama* oan that auld 78
She's the best leg a lamb oan the perfect plate
She's that extra fiver 'tae see ye awright'
She's *Dave Allan Oan Seturday Night*
She's ma wee maw

by Eddie Mc

Bingo

The bingo yins parked oan the step again
Clashin aboot the latest sanctionesses
Stoap it! Leave her alane!
Culture is the vulture.

Fag ash smears the different colours of cotton
Laughin' loud as they ridicule the skint.
The cheek ay them, they're rotten.
Tissues fur issues.

Facial hair n plooks compete fur space.
Yon arises tae attend tae the cries n flies.
That yin picks wine ower her weans.
No seen – no dream.

by BK

I am Smolt

I am
Smolt,
son of Salmon;
who needs to swim, chase, feed;
who loves flies, snails and worms
who hates noise, shadows and cannibal parents;
who fears fishermen, drought and getting lost;
who dreams of the sea, of shrimps and sprats;
who finds himself heading towards the open sea,
to grow
greatly,
to become Grilse.

by DT

Roach

I can't for the life of me tell you that I am good. But nor can I say that I am evil. You will have to judge me for yourself.

I was wandering around the kitchen trying to find a meal. I don't eat much, but still, no luck. I walked across the old wooden table and over that stupid slippery black and white chequered tiled floor. Everything was so disgustingly clean. And nothing in the room matched. Yellow fridge? Dark green cabinets.? Light blue walls? I mean who the hell doesn't match their stuff up these days? Right then the owner walked in and caught me hairy handed or footed. (or whatever the phrase is). He was a tall bony old guy, with a white beard, and dressed in hospital striped pyjamas. I could tell he didn't like the look of me from the start. He walked straight back out again. I had no idea what he was going to do but I headed towards the back door to leave. I mean, I didn't want to be an inconvenience to anyone.

Then he came bursting back in, wearing these big muddy old boots, dungarees with the straps hanging down to his ankles, but still in his pyjama jacket. He looked like something straight out of some American horror psycho film! And he was holding a huge double-barrelled shot gun. I know I'm big, but this gun was ridiculous. I thought I was done for.

But I have this real survival instinct – all my folks have it – and as I heard the trigger snap, I shuffled quickly to the side. *Bang.* I checked all my arms and legs. I was still in one piece. But there was a huge crater in the tiled floor. The old man's lips tightened. My being alive had just made him even more angry and he began to reload. I decided that the best form of defence was attack, so I ran up the inside of his dungarees – his hairy legs gave me an excellent grip – under his jacket, down his sleeve, and bit him on his old liver spotted hand. He yelled, the gun dropped, going off as it hit the ground.

The yellow fridge, the dark green cabinets and his black and white chequered tile floor that never matched up, looked even weirder now they were speckled red and purple.

I ran as fast as my legs would carry me, under the table, down the enormous wooden staircase, out through the crack at the bottom of the back door, across the treacherous gravel path, through the grass jungle and into the field of high crops, until I reached the safety of a discarded burger box, well away from the old man's place. And as I chewed on the remnants of a two week old Big Mac, watching the sun rise over the farm, I wondered when it would be safe enough to move back in.

by Anon

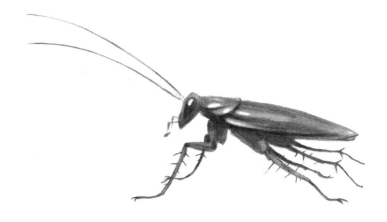

The Strangers

I look out my kitchen window and wonder, *who is this strange man in my garden?* He looks at me and I duck behind the wall. I say to myself, *it's my house, why am I hiding?* I'm thinking, *should I phone the police?* Where's my Sadie? I wonder if I should put my army medals on. That will show the scoundrel who's brave. I shout out, *Sadie get my medals!* Where is she? She would know what to do. My god he's coming up my garden path to the doorway as if it's his own bloody house, the scoundrel. Don't act scared. Be strong. Just like the army days. Look straight through him. How bloody dare he? Oh no, he's opening the door. He's opening the door! Stay calm. Stay calm. Here he comes. He's walking into my kitchen and looking right at me.

* * *

Oh god, he's ducking behind the kitchen window. I don't know if I can cope with this today. He's slipped into one of his episodes. God I hope it's one where he remembers me. Why does he always remember mum and not me? Dear old mum passed away years ago. I cannot muster enough patience to go through another sergeant major episode. Bloody embarrassing, trying to make me do press ups for answering back. Right, here's the door. Deep breath. Open it. And *be nice.*

"Hello dad, how are you keeping today?"

by J.R. Duffy

Midnight Breeze

A song

There's no -one outside;
it's just the wind blowing in the trees.
No, there's no-one outside;
it's just the midnight breeze.

There's nothing there,
just the sound of dead leaves.
No there's nothing there;
it's just the wind in the trees.

You can feel the cold within the room,
you can feel the rising moon,
shining down like a broken sun,
so we can see what we've become.

There's no-one outside;
it's just the wind blowing in the trees.
No, there's no-one outside;
it's just the midnight breeze.

There's nothing there,
just the sound of dead leaves.
No, there's nothing there;
it's just the midnight breeze.

by Anon

Kitchen School

Aged eight, I ate my
twelve times table.
Spooning forgotten soup,
watching coloured felt tip
numbers, recited by wide eyes.
And now the test.
the tables turned, what
have I learned?
Hands on trembly knees,
I see you purple hands: a
wooden spoon: your
knuckles white.
Seven eights are fifty six.
Eleven times would cloud my mind
and break the rhyme.
The spoon would speak, whack
it went and once again.
I'd turn, not cry, sometimes,
and learn.

by GK

Once upon a Time: a Fairytrial

"Stand up!" the Judge barked.

The small golden-haired girl stood up and looked anxiously around the courtroom.

"You are charged with breaking and entering," continued the judge, "with theft and with the wilful destruction of property. How do you plead girl?"

"Please, your honour," whimpered the girl, "I got lost. I didn't mean it! I'm sorry"

"Enough" the Judge snapped, "Just answer the question! Guilty or not guilty!"

"Not guilty your honour."

"Right, then let's get this moving," said the Judge, "Call the first witness."

There was a loud deep growl from behind which made her jump, and a large brown bear got to his feet and squeezed its great hairy bulk in to the witness box.

"What is your name?" said the Judge

"Mister Bear, your honour."

"Right Mister Bear, in your own time, please tell the court exactly what happened."

"Well your, honour," said Mister Bear, "My wife and I, Mrs Bear, had just made our breakfast porridge, like we always do, when we heard a loud howl coming from the forest. Naturally, being curious, myself, my wife and our little baby bear went out to see what it was. We couldn't see anything unusual, but better safe than sorry, so we went next door to our neighbours…."

"And who are were these neighbours Mister Bear?"

"Em, The Three Little Pigs, your honour,"

"The Three Little Pigs, thank you. Please continue Mister Bear."

"Well your honour, The Three Little Pigs said they hadn't

heard anything either, but also to be on the safe side, they decided to completely rebuild their straw house.

"Mister Bear, please tell the court what materials The Three Little Pigs rebuilt their house with!"

"Sticks, your honour. Good sturdy sticks."

"Thank you, the court will take note, please continue."

"Well your honour, we all went back home and that's when we made our first shocking discovery. Mister Bear stopped, his big paws were trembling, "Someone had been eating our porridge your honour. They'd taken a spoonful from my bowl and my wife's bowl but as for baby bear's bowl, they'd scoffed the lot! And if that wasn't bad enough, when I looked around I saw that someone had been sitting in each of our chairs, my big chair, Mrs Bear's medium sized chair and baby bears little chair."

"And how did you know this Mister Bear?"

"Because, your honour, baby bear's chair was broken in pieces."

There was loud murmuring in the public gallery.

"After that your honour, we thought we should go upstairs and check the bedrooms. Well, it was clear that someone had been sleeping in my bed, and also in my wife's bed. But then when we went into baby bear's bedroom, we discovered that the intruder was still there, fast asleep sleeping in baby bear's bed!"

"And can you see the person who was asleep in baby bear's bed in this room today Mr Bear?"

"Yes, your honour I can."

"Will you please point out the person to the court."

Mr Bear pointed to the young girl with the golden locks, "That's her, your honour."

"Thank you, Mister Bear, that must have been very stressful. You can go and sit down"

The judge looked at the young golden-haired girl over the top of his spectacles and spoke to her in a very harsh tone of voice,

"Well young lady, what do you have to say for yourself!"

With tears in her eyes, the little girl looked up at the judge. She spoke in a nervous whisper,.

"I was just … lost … and scared… your honour….and very *very* tired.

"And that's your excuse for breaking and entering, is it?"

The girl just nodded without saying another word.

"Miss Goldilocks," barked the Judge, "I find you guilty and sentence you to three years in prison. Take her away!"

As Goldilocks was taken down, the Judge turned to the clerk,

"Right, what is the next case?"

"Your honour," said the clerk, "it's the case of The Three Little Pigs, charged with the murder of a Mister B.B Wolf.

by Anon

wart hog

tiger in long grass
wart hog knows to get going
taxi time for him

by AD

I Am That Thought

I am that thought, the one in your head,
that thought that tells you to go back to bed.
I am the danger that lurks in the grass,
that thought that cannot be tamed by concrete and glass,
that thought, the keeper of the past.
I am that thought.
I am that thought, the one that likes to spoil your fun,
that thought that eclipses your sun,
that thought delivered at the point of a gun.
I am that thought.
I am that thought you cannot hold on to,
that thought that connects me to you
that thought that only feels safe to think at night,
that's afraid to come out
into the light.
I am
that thought.

by DG

MTV – a rap

Modern Western culture,
the economic vulture,
empty and bland,
people common as sand.
Money and image,
acceptance all the rage

Sport, a weekly tribal event,
where devotion and loyalty are misspent.
To play for the team,
the majorities dream,
the great atmosphere,
where you share joy and fear.

The peak of this spiral
is to get yourself viral.
Half your salary on fashion,
it's the corporate distraction
but try to buck the trend,
only one lifetime to spend

Are you *really* cool?
Or just a brainwashed fool?

by AD

Hai K.O

he ducks and punches
opponent is knocked out clean
belt risen over head.

by J.R. Duffy

Saved by Your Presence

A song

I've been saved by your presence
I've been bathed in your essence
And your stay's been a blessin'
Cos you made that impression

If you don't know by now
I'm going to show you how

I have strayed from the lesson
I have played and been messin'
That you came's been a pleasure
Now it's plain you're a treasure

If you don't know by now
I'm going to show you how

Shine a light by your window
Fine and bright while the wind blows

You have made world attention.
So your name needs no mention
That you came was refreshin'
And you made that impression

If you don't know by now
I'm going to show you how

Shine a light by your window
Fine and bright while the wind blows

by Tony M

Hurry Up and Boil

Hurry up and boil! Christ you're slow.

Hello, auld Mrs Wilson's got her washin oot. My God, you could camp in those knickers.

One spoon for me, one for the pot, and the one that got away. Are you no aboot ready tae whistle yet?

Must do something about that garden. Hard these days. Takes me all ma time jist to scratch ma erse let alone dig sods and pick spuds.

Had this kettle God knows how long. Aye, yer like me. Yer days are nearly up. Must get one of those new-fangled electric ones.

At last! So you've decided to boil have you?

A nice *Rich Tea* this morning ah think. Had the chocky ones yesterday.

That's it. Stir. Then strain. Aye, nothing beats a good strong cuppa. One sugar. Two sugar. Dollop a milk. At last. Mmm. Time tae sit doon. Feet up. Dunk the biscuit. Aah. Lovely.

(A short time later.)

Granddad wake up ye auld fool.

Whit?

You've gone and let your tea go cold ...again.

by Anon

All I want...

All I want is to be a mad inventor,
to change the world forever.
All I want is to create a big fuss,
to make explosions,
to make big clouds of dust.
All I want is to be a mad inventor,
to create a machine,
to make everlasting ice cream,
to fulfil every dream
All I want is to be a mad inventor,
to show off my gadgets in a whopping space centre.
All I need is to show no fear,
to proceed with the next big idea.
All I want is to be a mad inventor.

by AD

Barking Up the Wrong Tree

Christ.
How do you do it?
Why won't you leave?

Racing through my mind,
marking your territory
like a puppy.

Addicted to your smile,
finding myself at your beck and call,
like a dog.

Idly standing by,
unaware of the effect you have,
unaware of how much I care.

Gazing stupidly,
at those big blues.
Barking up the wrong tree.

by CR

Days on The Street

I remember my days on the street,
the city life and the pulsing beat,
an ounce of the bounce and dancing feet;
and the heat,
I remember the heat.

I remember chasing the dragon down destiny's lane
marking the tracks of a runaway brain,
pumping the blood through a varicose vein;
and the pain,
the pleasant pain

I remember running along in my race to be free,
tripping the switch of a mystery,
tasting the sweetness of ecstasy;
never to be,
it was never to be.

I remember the smoke in a curl,
turning the sky to a mother of pearl,
high in the clouds with my head in a whirl;
and a girl,
a golden girl

Where are you now, as I grow old?
Nowhere to run, no Colombian gold,
Nowhere to cry as my heart grows old;
it's time to fold,
it's time to fold.

> I'm only alive in my memory's eye,
> a ghost in the dust of days gone by,

No-one to help,
I don't know why;
it's time to die,
it's time to die

by Anon

And Every Time I Hear That Song

Every time I hear that song
I'm reminded that it's been so long
since I saw you.

Summer days drinking in the park,
not getting home 'til after dark,
smoking weed and watching telly
rubbing our old pitbull's belly.

And every time I hear that song.

Every time I hear that song
I'm reminded that it's been so long
since I saw you.

Razor Light stuck on repeat,
drinking *Captain Morgan* neat,
tiny high-tops at my front door,
never to be seen, no more.

And every time I hear that song.

by Anon

Heartbeats

Your little heart beats, beating,
beating, fast it goes,
like a drum roll
beats, repeating.
Echoes,
echoing from an ultrasound.

Your picture, vague, blurred,
on that screen,
is the clearest picture
I've ever seen.

by Anon

The Massacre

(an overheard conversation in a café)

Man In Hat: There was twelve a them. I couldnae haud back.
Ah destroyed every single wan a them. Total massacre.

Man In Scarf: Yer jokin! No way! (*Impressed*) Ah don't know
how ye dae it big man.

Man In Hat: Ye know me. First ah rip their heeds right aff.
Then ah target the legs. Ah pure love it. (…) Aye, ah pure
love ginger bread men.

by GS

The Urchin

The cold bites
on brightest nights
when a quilt of leaves
is removed by breeze
under the Hedge

A warm bed
the boy has fled,
holds only fears.
Floods of tears
inside his head.

Dawn has found
the fair in town.
Laughs and screams,
fruit machines
'til closing down

Sun has shone
crowds have gone.
The world's asleep,
it's time to creep
under the Hedge

by GK

The Cathkin Braes

this is where me and ma pals wid come
when ah was a wean,

fields fu' a' colour
trees aw staunin in line
green fields n bracken
wee streams runnin this wey n that
paths twistin and turnin.
walkin aimless fur oors oan end
listenin tae aw the birdsongs
an me
jist breathin it aw in

by Eddie Mc

This Is The Hard Core Life – a brief extract

This is the hard-core life. The question that many asked those who knew him was, *When did his life start to go bad?* The honest answer, there was never a time that he considered it to be good. Forget about *happy*, he never even got to *okay*. It was always going to end messy, a tired inevitability about the finish. The main problem with the deeply wounded is, how do you rid yourself, from those who terrorised you? Who continue to haunt you, even after they die? What advice do you give someone who is determined to self-destruct? Who resents not having a major role, in the game of life? Who has to satisfy themselves with a silent cameo appearance? Whose name, does not rate a mention in the closing credits?

How do we deal with all that unfilled potential in our world? The graveyards are littered with such people. Most of them died prematurely. Let us explore the descent into madness, the chaos and the self-loathing that usually results in an early death.

1996. Another year of living precariously.

I am not just having a bad day, month, or year. It is a bad life filled with days of wine and poses. Death waits patiently on a bench across the street. I believe I will not see forty. No, I am *determined* not to see forty. I hit the prison system two years previous. One six-month sentence, then another. I've grown to dislike prison; the place has become too familiar. Law and order finally lost patience with me. *Trouble* is now my routine. Life is spiraling out of control. The ghost of future prison sentences, looms in the foreground.

I've done a Geographic, moving away from the metropolis, trying to be less conspicuous, spending a number of months, in a dysfunctional relationship in a small country town in the wheat belt. My alcoholism ... Did I mention I was an alcoholic, or did you take it for granted – is far more noticeable now. It provides ammunition for the rumour merchants, trading in slur. But that's typical in miniscule populations. The fact that my partner 'W' is indigenous, fuels the redneck, yokels, within this -still segregated -community. Snide remarks and disgusted glances assault me wherever I go, declaring me 'guilty' of being a traitor to my race. This town throws me backwards in time. I half expect the local Klu Klux Klan, to pelt our house with Molotov cocktails, and burning crosses, to appear on the lawn.

It's a carbon copy, of towns across the country. A monstrous art colonial oldveau, two storey hotel on the corner of main street, two banks, a general store, a bowling club, police station, health centre, football oval. That's it. Same conversations too. The weather, the football club, marriages, affairs, divorce, birth, death, the crop yield, the party, the dwindling numbers at Church. Blah, blah, blah. Entertainment is limited; the Country Women's Association cake stall, the annual barn dance. It's a hick town, stuck in a time warp of the 1950s white policy, a racist satellite of the British empire, where the indigenous were – are – not even considered citizens. Here, apartheid exists. Indigenous people are still segregated, still living in a shanty-town, still effectively excluded from pubs, clubs and without any local council influence or community role.

Back to 'W'. I had met her on a drunken weekend, while still in a relationship with 'F', who at the time was being held captive in a Psych ward where she spent her days reliving her traumatic childhood. 'F' seemed to be forever in some sort of therapy. Our relationship alone probably ensured at least a decade's worth. She was being held in a private institution; psychiatry for the pampered, inventive in their handing out of designer labels, disorders tailor made to an upper-class clientele.

Being unfaithful is par for the course. It's the least shocking thing you will hear in this miserable tale. Despite this 'F' is still the idealized love of my life. My soul-fate. Losing her will precipitate a sharp decline. I will give up on happiness. 'F' continued to play on my heartstrings long after the concert ended. What was the attraction? Her pain. I wanted to heal her. And felt lingering guilt, as I wounded her further.

'W' and I were the classic alcoholic partnership, sharing a love of – above all else – the bottle. But we weren't isolated small town drunks. Competition came in the form of a fifty year old former matron. She drank with us, passed out with us, and fought with us as we all projected our anger and disgust at our personal predicament onto each other and the world. So it was, day in day out. It was an alcoholic Ground Hog Day, with 'W' desiring permanence and yours truly looking for a way out. She is insanely jealous and I'm her prized possession. Any mention of other females is regarded as total betrayal and often ends in violence. I still have the bite mark on my arm, my souvenir of that relationship. I didn't retaliate. I found it amusing. *What have I signed up for this time* I thought. Can a life get any more pathetic than the one I am living? Watch this space.

by C

the wee numpty

the wee numpty
looking for a fix
that wee numpty
pulling tricks

steals your wallet
nicks your car
caught by the cops
never gets far

mugging, misery
where ever he goes
because he's stupid
it's all he knows

but, take a chance
teach him something new
you never know
he might surprise you

by Anon

Timidity

Timidity is a hiding dog,
creeping behind the couch,
slouched;
leaving just enough room
to observe
his haven from harm,
only coming out when he's alone

A past life may explain,
the hidden scars,
the pain

Timidity
is his chain

by Anon

Tipple

for every man
a tipple is a little
thirst for home

by BK

Peh

Peh.
greasy n squishy
boilin n steamin n munchin.
teckle piece o' creeshie peh.
half time delight.

by Anon

mouth hug

granny's apple pie
good childhood memories
gives your mouth a hug

by J.R. Duffy

In a Parallel Universe

In a parallel universe:
I found the chimps that typed out the complete works of
    Shakespeare; it was infinitely strange;
gave Schrodinger's cat a saucer of milk, it drank the lot and
    ignored it;
flew from a black hole, eyes shielded from the glare;
met myself and argued.

by GK

Snow Angels and Snow Men

A silent cacophony of crows dominate,
iron and gunpowder lace the air, now
a blanket of innocence: no man's land,
as children make angels and men from snow.

Saint Christopher, stranded, weeps from afar;
tiptoe   like taking your first steps, again,
bleeding footprints betray ghostly secrets,
as children make angels and men from snow.

From ice graves, naked branches twist and
turn; reaching, calling, for loved ones   long gone,
like wild skeletons trapped in a snow globe,
as children make angels and men from snow.

A silent cacophony of crows dominate,
as children make angels and men from snow

by CR

Killie Bus Tales

(The Number 11)

Ah'm sittin upstairs oan the number eleven.
Ther's four neds behind me – two men, two wumin,
drinkin cans a *Super* n *Frosty Jacks.*
(ah wish ah hudnae sat sae close tae the back)
The men -in identical trackies, trainers n hair-
ur bad-mouthin mates who urnae ther
n squeezin the cans tae get aw the dregs
n moanin aboot the queues in the chemist n *Greggs.*
The wumin are talkin aboot due dates n lib dates
n they've crumbs oan their chins frae yesterdays steak bakes.
Wan's visitin her man who's in the jail;
the dad's his best mate who's oot oan bail.
(Nothin tae worry aboot fur a while
then it'll aw get sorted oot …oan *Jeremy Kyle*)
Ther's a commotion noo comin up the stair;
some guy wi a baseball cap n his burd wi red hair.
Him in *Crosshatch, Voi* n fake *Stone Island,*
her cerryin six carrier bags fae *Farmfoods* n *Iceland,*
eyes hawf closed n skin coloured leggins
fu' a the blues n gabapentin.
Tho' her haunds are full n she's in some state,
she still manages a moothfa of her *Frijj* milk shake.
She barks oot the order, "Mek me a roll-up Steven,"
as a voice fae behind shouts,
"Here mate, yer burd looks like Ed Sheeran!"

by GB

The Foxford Shrimp

Tagged oval silver,
tail of red breast feather,
wound to perfection;
like lucky white heather.

Body of seals fur,
fiery-brown and black,
oval silver ribbed,
from front to back.

Cheeks of jungle cock,
hackle of rich ginger,
red whipped finished head;
perfect for a *Springer*.

by DT

Old Nick and the Lottery Winner

(Inspired by a Mayan folk tale)

Once upon a time, there was an Edinburgh man who did the lottery week in, week out, year after year. He'd never won as much as a pound and he was mighty sick of not winning. Now, next week was a hundred-million-pound rollover. "I'll never win", he said to himself. But then, he had an idea, "At midnight I'll go to the crossroads where the Royal Mile meets Surgeons Hall and I'll do a deal with Old Nick himself."

And that's what he did. That night as the clock struck twelve, the man arrived at the crossroads.

"Come forth Old Nick!" he shouted out. Nothing happened. "I have a deal for you!" But still Old Nick did not appear. The man was desperate to win the lottery, so he fell to his knees and tried again. "Grant me this wish and my soul will be yours forever." Still nothing! The man rose to his feet, dejected. But when he looked around, who should be standing there but his own father, who had been dead these past twelve years.

"Dear God in Heaven!," cried the man. "Is that you father?"

"No, I'm not your father," said the man, smiling, "It's Old Nick who stands before you! I've taken this form because I thought it would be easier for you. I can change into something else if you'd prefer. Pamela Anderson maybe?" He laughed at his joke, then immediately became deadly serious, "Or perhaps you'd prefer to see my true form?"

"No, no, not your true form," the man cried out, "Stay as my father, please."

"That's just as well," laughed Old Nick, "because no one except God himself can look upon my true form and live to tell the tale. Now then, remind me, why have you summoned me?"

"I want to win the lottery."

"And to achieve that, you are willing to sell me your soul?"

"Yes, exactly." Old Nick just stood there with his hands in his pockets. "So…what do I need to do?"

"Just shake my hand and whatever numbers you come up with will be the winning numbers."

"And that's it?"

"That's it.. Oh…and just after you've won, I'll pop round to your house to collect your soul."

Well the man shook Old Nick's hand and as he walked home, he began thinking of all the amazing things he would do with his millions. He did wonder about Old Nick getting his part of the deal, but it didn't worry him too much,

"Why would I need a soul, when I'll have a hundred million pounds to keep me happy?"

When he got home, he called his twin brother. He told him that he was going to be coming into a large amount of money.

"I'll take you for a few pints bro'. Then we can come back to my place for a takeaway and watch the lottery draw on telly."

Well, the twin wondered what was going on. He and his brother had always fought like cat and dog. Why was he deciding to share his good fortune now? But, never one to turn down a free meal, he agreed.

Well they went to the pub and the man bought his twin endless pints and whisky chasers – while the man himself just sipped on the same one pint all night. By the time they got back to the flat, the twin brother was steaming drunk, and fast asleep on the settee, and the lottery draw was just starting on the telly.

Just as Old Nick had predicted, the man had just won a hundred million pounds. The man was delighted and immediately he snuck off behind the settee, leaving his sleeping drunk twin sitting on his own. Moments later, Old Nick in the shape of the father appeared on the television screen and believing the drunk sleeping twin to be the man, began to suck the soul from out of him. But no matter how hard he tried the soul would not come out. Old Nick was so furious, he turned back into his true self, but fortunately the twin was asleep, and the brother was behind the settee so neither of them set eyes on him. Well, eventually Old Nick gave up and left to do some business elsewhere. The drunk twin carried on asleep on the settee, unaware of all that had happened, while his brother was a hundred million pounds better off, and all the happier for outwitting Old Nick himself!

by Anon

First love saves my life

First nervous glance, the flutter of my heart,
Your eyes meet mine; your beauty sets you apart.
Short and sweet are the walks down the beach.
Want to hold you close, but you are just out of reach.

First friends, then lovers, the months fly by.
Know you a lot better and the things that make you cry.
Desires get urgent, wait for when we next meet.
My dreams are to be with you, my life is so sweet.

First time at the altar, standing in awe of your presence,
I swear to stand by you, pure picture of innocence.
Work hard to provide for you, to be always beside you,
The way you smile, your sigh, the things that you do.

As time goes on, memories drift away,
but your love keeps me alive, to this very day.

by Anon

The Hope Good People Bring

I have the skin I am in.
My febrile tears
belie the good years

I open my eyes.
Shroud-like shadows hang
waiting in my darkness

I scream to see
all the beauty
once placed in front of me

If I listen
I can hear my breath
and a glimmer returns

Slowly, surely
smaller yet clearer
flesh jewels inspire the light.

by Anon

The Last Cigarette

(after William Carlos Williams & Tom Leonard)

This just to say
I have smoked
the last cigarette
that was on the mantelpiece
and which
you were keeping
for yourself

forgive me
it was magic
so stress relieving
and so worth it

by DG

blud oan the flair

the blud,
it wiz a' gushin.

the flair wiz covird,
ma heed wiz buzzin,
ma da wiz goin
oan n oan

ma ma
she telt me
yer *da winna belt ye,*
jiz go an clean
the flair

by Anon

Inch High

If I were only one inch high
I'd float up to the sky
on a soapy bubble,
and *pop*,
I'd fall to the ground
and splash.
into a puddle.

I'd sail ashore on a twig,
with a leaf for a sail,
and hitch a lift
on a turbo charged snail
If I were only one inch high.
If I were only one inch high.

by Anon

If I Was A Bird

If I was a bird
I'd soar above the tallest trees,
I'd swoop down on rivers and woods
and dine on fish and bees.
I'd holiday in the south of France
(and mate with an exotic hummingbird –
if I got the chance!)
If I was a bird
If I was a bird

by Anon

A Letter Found in a Dead Man's Pocket

People in my country call my issue "sickness or madness". Of course, I'm not sick or mad.

Since my teenage period has begun, my life has turned out to be a life from hell.

When I was a child I didn't exactly know what was the difference between women and men. It was the same to me. I played with girls or with boys and didn't care whether I was a male or a female. But when I turned seventeen, some strange changes began. Every day was the same, I would stand in front of the mirror and repeat the same questions.

I was living like a stranger in my own world and I found myself in mental isolation and painful loneliness inside my family. There were some moments I wasn't sure anymore if I knew my friends, teachers, streets or even my relatives.

No longer did anything seem normal to me. Every single moment I had a hurt feeling like a sharp knife was twisting in the bottom of my heart. And serious questions kept repeating in my head:

Why I'm created like this? What are these unwelcome changes in my body? What is happening to my voice? Why is it so raised-thick and awful? What are these additional organs between my legs? It's indeed a congenital defect! The best idea is to cut them off.

That was my life's secret, my deep-continuous suffering and I had to face it alone.

Who can I blame? Who should I talk to? Parents? Imams? Psychologists and doctors? No way! Neither these nor those would understand my issue. I know exactly what's in the box. No one going to stand up for me or back me up. So, I didn't have any intention to talk to anyone.

I am a woman.

There is no doubt about it and I am really tired of living as a man. I want to be what I really am.

I want to wear a dress or skirt. I want to put on earrings, necklaces, bracelets and high-heeled shoes. I want to have a huge breasts and long black hair as my twin sister has. I want to have a slim-smooth and elegant figure. I want to do my hair, face, lips and finger-and toe nails.

I want to work as a child care manager or a house keeper and the top of my dreams is getting married, being pregnant, having a baby and breastfeeding him or her.

I want to be a wife. I can't imagine myself as a husband. I am a woman's soul in a man's body.

I want to be who I am.

One day, my twin sister walked into the kitchen and heard me talking in front of the mirror. I didn't know that she heard me. She said nothing and continued preparing her tea.

by AA

128

My City

This is Glesga. Or Glasgow!
It depends on how the name rolls aff yer tongue or
whit housin scheme ye were brought up in.
But tae me, ma city is Glesga.

This is ma city.
When terrorists attacked oor airport,
we fought back.
They'll think twice aboot attackin oor city again.
Why? Cos we will set aboot ye!

This is ma city.
When the helicopter crashed oan oor *Clutha Vaults* pub
oor people stood up tae be counted.
They ran towards the burnin buildin
tae pull their fellow Glaswegians oot.
Why? Cos this is Glesga!

This is ma city.
It will welcome aw strangers n immigrants!
Oor girls fae Drumchapel fought the establishment n won.
Why? Cos this is Glesga.

by J.R. Duffy

Look! Don't Look!

Look my way if you're honest and kind,
Don't look my way if you're full of yourself.
Look my way and I'll share with you
Don't look my way to greet me with smugness,
Don't look my way to tell me of your millions
Look my way to share your wisdom
Don't look my way to bad mouth others
Don't look my way to sit about team handed
Don't look my way to join you in taking liberties
Look my way and I'll be loyal to you
Don't look my way to ponce and ponce
Don't look my way then go to hell
Don't look my way if you want an enemy
Look my way for a friend of the easy life

by BK

Murphy

My bull terrier, Murphy, is definitely psychic.
There is so much wisdom behind the eyes of my
warrior side-kick. When I'm feeling blue, he knows
what to do. He nuzzles me with his big boulder
head and licks my face til I get out of bed. One look
from him, says a thousand words. I just wish he would
learn to pick up his turds.

by Anon

Approaching Full Circle

Louise entered the cemetery. It was a cool, calm summer's night with no one around except the occasional dog walker. She'd been through three years of anger and blame since she broke up with John. This was only her second time here. She found it soothing the first time, but she could only muster the courage to visit once a year.

John was sitting perched on the end of the bench next to the grave. Louise sat down on the opposite end, as far away from him as she could possibly be. She stared for a while at the neatly cut grass, then stood up abruptly and started throwing away the dead flowers and generally tidying up the grave.

"Oh I see you do you have a bit of decency left in you," said John, his voice dripping with sarcasm.

Louise ignored him. She sat back down, and leaned forward and started to cry,

"I'm sorry John, I really am. I honestly didn't know. I swear to god."

"Fuck sake," said John. "You said all this last time."

That night in his cell when he was remanded back into custody, he'd sworn never to forgive her, but she was here beside him, and he had a strong urge to comfort her. An old woman walked by with her dog. As it growled in John's direction, the woman saw Louise was in tears,

"You okay hen?"

Louise nodded. The dog was barking now, pulling on the leash, towards John.

"I'm sorry about Buttons," she said, "I don't know what's got into him today." As she walked away the dog was still barking at John and straining at the leash.

"I hate dogs," said John.

"Dogs have never been keen on you," said Louise, managing a smile.

"Ah, so you can smile after all I see."

He was scared to look into those gorgeous blue eyes. It wouldn't take much to forget his anger and fall back under her spell.

"Thanks for not telling your mum and the police what really happened." He would've said more had a grey pit-bull pup not appeared from nowhere.

"C'mere son," said Louise, immediately cooing over the pup, "you're a lovely wee dog, aren't you."

"Why do people speak to dogs as if they're babies?" said John

Louise carried on playing with the dog. It made her laugh. It made John feel the rush of an emotion he hadn't felt for a very long time – happiness. It wasn't ever her he had hated, it was the pain.

A man clutching a dog lead, ran up to Louise.

"Oh thanks hen," he said, "you're a life-saver. I thought I lost him there."

"He's a wee cracker. What's his name?"

"Mick." The man turned to go, but then stopped, "I'm Derek by the way. Look, I don't mean to be cheeky," he said, "but did you not used to go out with John Murn?"

"Yeah," said Louise.

Derek put the lead back on the dog and sat down on the bench between her and John.

"I heard what happened," said Derek, "but you know, you have to learn to move forward, get on with your life."

"Funny you should say that, but just today I felt that a large burden had been lifted just by coming here to say goodbye."

"Goodbye?"

"I'm moving away tomorrow. Fresh start."

"I'm sorry," said John, "maybe it's time for me to go too."

And as John melted away into the summer night air, Louise got up and left.

"Good on you hen," Derek shouted after her, "And good luck."

The pup wandered over to the gravestone and started

sniffing around it. Derek grabbed the lead and glanced at the name on the stone. John Murn .

"See Mick," said the man, "that's the guy we were just talking about."

by R.J. Duffy

My Life as a Ghost

In the afterlife I will return as a ghost and haunt all those who done me wrong. Some, I will freak out just short of the point of insanity. Others, I'll just have some fun with; move objects, make them feel very uncomfortable, that sort of thing. Then, once I've had my fun I will sit back and enjoy some of the "ghost" stories they'll tell about me and laugh when nobody believes them.

But, until then… BOO!

by Anon

One man's pain is another man's laughter.

It was a Tuesday night, early February 1997. I was head chef at a twenty-six-bedroom family-owned Hotel in Kirkcaldy and busy prepping up for the service.

"Stuart!" a waitress shouted out, "Phone for you!"

It was mum. She was upset.

"Stuart when's your days off this week?"

"Wednesday or Thursday mum why?"

"I have just got the *Fife Leader*. Dave McN has passed away."

"God, that's a shame mum."

Davie was a good pal of my dad's. He was at his funeral, ten years ago.

"His funeral is tomorrow. Will you go and pay the respects of the family?"

"Yes, no problem. Look I have to go now, we have a big service tonight."

"Okay son. I'll have your suit all ironed and ready."

Service went well and as usual as we cleaned down at half ten. My adrenalin was pumping. Tuesday night was wages night. I went into the hotel bar and had my first pint. The owners were a nice couple who allowed you one sweat pint for free. The receptionist came through with my wages, cash money, in a little brown packet. I checked my wage slip and tallied in. The first pint hardly touched the sides, so I ordered another. There were seven or eight staff in the bar, so I asked them if they wanted a drink, and usual they all took me up on my offer. The second pint was just as nice as the first. My intention was to finish it and head straight home. Ah, the best laid plans. Just as I took my last gulp, another came over. What had I started?

We all ended up chatting, about music. *The Stone Roses*,

Oasis or *Blur*, and where did *Pulp* fit into this equation? Just at that, my sous chef, came over with yet another pint.

"Heh, I have a funeral in the morning."

"Don't worry it's no yours."

Last orders were rung. I was literally saved by the bell. But when I look round, lo and behold there's four gin and tonics sitting there, calling out my name. We sat in until well past shutting time, setting the world to rights. At some point somebody must have called me a taxi. I remember arriving home but not much of the journey.

I was awoken the next morning with a mixture of my alarm clock and my mum yelling.

"Stuart! You're going to be late for the funeral!"

I opened one eye and glanced at the clock. 8.42am. I sprung out of bed and raced to the bathroom.

"Mum!" I shouted, mouth full of toothpaste, "What time's the funeral?"

"Half-nine."

"Phone for a taxi right away."

I jumped in the shower and had a quick shave while mum got my clothes ready. Grey pinstripe suit, white shirt, black tie, black handkerchief. I couldn't get the knot in my tie right. Three times I tried and each time I got more and more frustrated.

"Come here," she said, like I was back at school. "I'll fix it."

Outside, the taxi was peeping the horn. 9.22am. I started to sweat. 'Oh no. I'm going to be late.' Luckily we were only a mile from Kirkcaldy crematorium.

There were hundreds of people waiting at the crematorium. Now, I'm only five feet three and I was standing right at the back. I looked around but I didn't recognise a single person. Everybody I know will be in the family cars, I thought; Davie, junior, his sons. I kept telling myself it's alright, it's been ten years since I lived in Smeaton, so it's natural I should forget a face or two.

The family car arrived, but went straight into the

crematorium and once again I couldn't catch a glimpse of them. Two of the crematorium staff started ushering people to seats on the left and right. I just went with the flow and ended up fourteen rows back, right in the middle. The family took up the front two rows but all I could see was the back of their heads.

Music played, we all stood up, and this Humanist celebrant comes in. This is strange, I thought. Davie's family were devout Catholics.

"We are here today," said the Humanist, "to celebrate the life of Shug as he was known to his family and Friends!" Shug? I'd never heard Davie McN called Shug before. But maybe it was one of those family nicknames. The Humanist continued, "Shug worked hard in the post office for many years." Post office? He was a *miner* alongside my dad!

"He loved to play the accordion to his grandkids."

Davie was tone deaf for fuck sake! He'd lost three fingers down the pit.

At this point my mouth dried up and my stomach ties itself in knots. I felt sick. The penny had dropped. I was at the wrong bloody funeral.

I looked at the doors. Closed. Anyway, I couldn't get up; there was people either side of me. There was no way out. It was a nightmare. Beads of sweat formed on my brow. Panic set in. I sat there frozen like a Meercat, praying – ironic I know – taking deep breaths, picking up bits and pieces about *Shug* from the service,

"Born in Lochgelly, Shug's first job was down the pit. That's where he met the love of his life, in the pit canteen. When she died five years ago, Shug was never quite the same, but he still enjoyed life surrounded by his doting family."

This Shug seemed a right decent guy. Then I started to think of my own dad, and now I was getting emotional as well as mortified. I was going in and out of panic. But I made a plan. At the end of the ceremony as everyone stood up to leave, I'd head off through the back door. Sorted.

The service drew to a close, "As you leave there will be a collection for cancer research, and you are all welcome to join the family afterwards."

That'll be right!

The curtains closed around the coffin and everyone stood. This was my opportunity. Or was it? Only the doors at the front were open. That was the only exit. And now the family were all lined up thanking people for coming. A woman in her forties introduced herself,

"Hi I'm Shugs daughter," she said, with a confused look on her face. "How did you know my dad?"

Think! Think! Breathe. Breathe.

"Oh," I says, "my dad worked with your dad. My mum asked me to come along and pay our respects.

"Can I ask who your dad was?"

"Wee Ecky."

She pondered for a moment, and then,

"Oh wee Ecky? I remember dad speaking of him. How kind of you and your mum after all these years." And then she shouts to the man next to her, in this broad fife accent, "This is wee Ecky's boy."

"Thanks for coming mate," he says. I just nod.

I stuck a tenner into the collection and stepped outside. It's was a proper Scottish winters day, dark skies and howling wind. Kirkcaldy crematorium was a well-oiled machine and the next funeral was already ready to go in. In amongst them I spotted Gary E and his sister, and Craig O' D, my old next-door neighbour. Then I had a light bulb moment. Davie's funeral was next.

I edged away from both sets of mourners and headed towards the main road, hoping and praying no one from Davie's funeral clocked me. As I headed for home the skies cracked and the heavens opened. Two family cars passed by heading towards the bypass, Shug's family. I put my head to the floor. I needed to get this nightmare of a morning over and done with. I heard a loud exhaust and blaring techno coming from behind, and as I turned around a white XR2 drove through a puddle and soaked me.

"Get it up ye," shouts the wee knob in the front, and he gives me the vicky, laughing as he drove off.

No more than an hour and a half had passed. When I left I was looking like a mannequin from *Slaters* shop window, but now soaked to the skin, I'm more like a miniature Duncan Goodhew.

When I got back mum was sitting in her chair next to the coal fire, *Senior Service* cigarette in one hand, rum and coke in the other,

"I'm just having a wee drink for Davie," she says, "how did it go?"

"How did it fucking go?" I says, "You sent me to the wrong bloody funeral! Davie's was the ten o' clock."

"It was 9.30 I'm telling you!" And adamant she's right she toddled through to the kitchen to get the *Fife Leader*, "Here it is," she says, opening the paper,

Low and behold, David McN, funeral, 10am, blah blah blah. It's a genuine mistake but that made me feel no better, and to rub salt in the wound, mum had started laughing.

"So why didn't you go to Davie's funeral after?"

I just stared at her.

A couple of weeks later mum asked me to go to the Post Office and collect her widow's pension, plus a copy of the *Fife Leader*. As I was waiting in the queue, who comes into the shop but young Davie McN. I felt I needed to explain to him how I had missed his dad's funeral and ended up telling him the whole story from start to finish. By the end Davie junior was in hysterics, tears of laughter rolling down his cheeks.

"Thanks so much Stuart," he says, "I really needed that. That's the most I've laughed since my dad passed away."

So, in the end I just thought, one man's pain is another man's laughter.

by S

Same Again Squire?

Same again Squire?
Aye make it a double.

Count out my cash, money goes fast.
I'll get back on the ale, brandy won't last.
I should spend some on food, my belly is yawning.
I've only had coffee and toast since this morning.

Here you go Squire, thy pint and thy double.

Along the bar, patrons laugh in huddles,
stools dragged, betting slips crumpled,
coins counted, tumblers clatter,
all's cosy, happy; nothing's the matter

Same again Squire? Thy pint and thy double?

It's almost eleven, I'm already in trouble.
Head for the toilets, should make it in time
Stumble into old Maggie, at the jukebox, *Patsy Cline.*
'Who's sorry now?' I get the meaning of that line.
If there's a queue for the urinal, the sink will do fine.

by DS

New Toy

I wasn't a man but wasn't a boy.
At the age of thirteen I found a new toy.
It wasn't like an *Action Man* or a ball.
It came by the name of alcohol.

Drinking to take away confusion and pain
Waking, confused and praying,
oh God,
I haven't made a fool of myself again?

by SB

A Lost Soul

When I was young it seemed like everyone in my housing scheme was learning to play the guitar. I tried to do the same. I learned all the chords, but I just couldn't get the hang of the rhythm. There was one guy in our scheme, Larry, who was excellent on most musical instruments and he could sing too. But Larry's story is also one of struggle, of hitting rock bottom due to drug and alcohol addiction. Then one Christmas Eve a crowd of us were on our way to midnight mass, when I bumped into him. He didn't look great. After a brief chat he decided to tag along. The chapel was packed, and it was a good service. Afterwards Larry said that he couldn't believe how much he had enjoyed it and said that he was going to start going every week. That night was the last time that Larry touched any form of alcohol. I know this because around six months later I bumped into him again and this time he looked a lot healthier and so self-assured. He invited me and some other folk to his house that weekend for a jam and a sing-along. He said we could bring alcohol if we liked as he was confident it didn't bother him anymore. I could hardly believe the change in him.

The weekend came and we went down to his house. When I walked into his living room, I couldn't believe my eyes. There, next to the window was the first grand piano I had ever seen, a gift from his parents to show how proud they were of him. Most of my friends had brought their guitars and some beverages and it wasn't long before Larry let us hear him on the piano. He was really good. At first, he just played well known songs while everyone took turns singing. There were a few right good chanters in our group, like you wouldn't believe.

But then Larry started singing some of his own songs, at times playing the guitar and harmonica or the piano, whilst others played guitar. Larry was now a proper all-round musician. In this short space of time he'd got CDs made of his own songs. Most of them he'd written during his drinking days, but some were about how he'd had dragged himself away from the booze and the drugs.

The night turned out to be brilliant. I'll end my tale here with this note; if Larry can turn his life around, then there's hope for us all.

by Anon

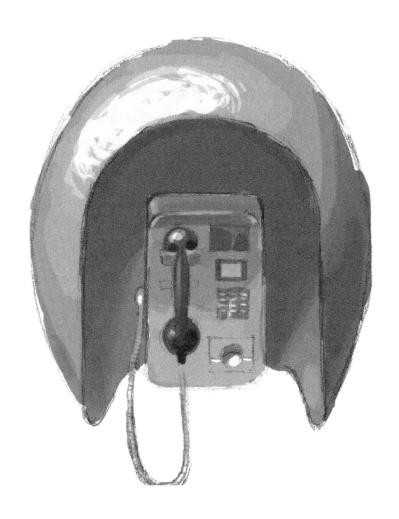

The Hotcheeks Squirrel

Tied on a size twelve hook,
goes a *tungsten bead* of gold,
the tail of *grey fox squirrel;*
a fly for March I'm told.

Body built with *squirrel dubbing,*
ribbed with *twinkle tinsel,*
that lights this little trout fly
like a Christmas angel.

Cheeks blush with red floss,
hackles from a partridge's neck.
Fish this upstream style,
or like a short-lined Czech.

by DT

The Ultimate High Horse

arrogance
is the superior unicorn,
trotting high above
on clouds in the sky.
looking down,
unique and wonderful

by AD

Sugar Coated Memories

Do you remember *Space Dust*
crackling on your tongue?
Or those gobstoppers
that left your jaw unsprung?
What about pink bubble gum
stuck across your face?
And furiously munching
a strawberry shoelace?
Mind shovelling 99's
with crumbly chocolate flakes?
A 10p mix up
and chewy jelly snakes?
It wasn't always fun.
Much I'd like to skip.
But I can still remember
the taste of sherbet dip.

by GK

rendezvous

sittin in the hoose / bored oot ma heid / telly's snide/ might go back tae bed / then the dug starts tae whimper n geez me that stare / get yer arse in gear daddy or ah'll shite oan yer flair / so ah jump tae ma feet n pull oan ma strides / the dug sterts tae bark n doon the loaby he slides / we're headin oot fur a walk / grab a slice a toast / mak oor way alang speirshall close / suns splittin the sky / the taps ur aff / cut oan tae the cycle path /the auld drinkers ur ther under dyke road pass / lazily bakin oan the grass /the doo flyers ur oot, cluckin n cooin oan the ridge / just when we approach the kingsway bridge / the dugs aff the leash / he bolts fur the doos / bangs intae the drinkers n knocks oor thir booze /stroll past the bookies oan dumbarton road /the toothless approach n try to lighten ma pocket load / arrive at the rendezvouz lounge n bar / plant oor weary arses n order a jar

by Anon

The Conversation

I wait in bed for the cell door to be opened. I can hear footsteps, the keys being jangled and then the bright white lights come on one by one. So bright. Brighter than a morgue. I feel like I'm under observation all the time. If it's not the officers in the hall it's the CCTV cameras all around. The minutes tick by. I can hear them laughing at some joke. Why don't they open us up? Is someone's cell going to be tossed by security? Is someone being 'moved' to the segregation? Or worse, the suicide cell. That would mean loud banging at all hours of the night! Finally, the door opens with a bang and I join the mad rush for the section phone. There are three of them in our section but only one can be relied on to work.

I'm in luck today. I reach the phone before anybody else. Under the cold grey cowling of the phone box I pick up the handset and start dialling. I barely need to look at the keys. Four years of dialling the same number has imprinted it onto my memory. It's the same ritual observed on a daily basis, the same number, the same urgency. The same bad connection, with that persistent buzzing in the background. The Big Brother Effect, as one paranoid inmate calls it. I wait for the pre-recorded message to kick in, wait to hear her voice, to know for sure if it's her who's picked up. The phone keeps ringing. "Pick up, pick up," I mutter.

I could hear a pin drop. I can feel the tension.

Hesitant greetings start my call. I try to remember what I'd last said, but I keep hitting a wall. I keep one eye on the notes that I scribbled down in haste, and the other eye on the phone, to make sure no credit goes to waste. Money slips through like time down an hourglass. The scratched LCD display makes it harder to guess. I hold tight the scuffed black handset. The scratched keys of the phone are making me quietly upset.

The phone grows warmer, my palms are sweating, my heartbeats grow louder. My head starts aching, then the pain spreads, enveloping me. Her voice breaks up, struggling to break free. I touch my forehead on the cold metal cowling to cool myself down. There are names etched on it, and a map, of a town. The laminated notice is covered in obscenities written in dust. The chewing gum stuck in the mesh makes me shudder with disgust.

All around me the noise of prisoners laughing and cheering, officers shouting, snooker balls rattling and table tennis balls being batted, echoes off the walls and drowns out my conversation. I want to withdraw into a shell with the phone in my hand. I just want some silence.

As soon as I retreat back into the dark silence of my cell, I try to remember the conversation I've just had, try to piece it back together. What were those last words? What did she say to me? What did she mean by that? Try to hold on to it a bit longer, to savour the sounds, the sighs, the laughter. Words that might stop me from going mad in this hell. But it's all been left behind. I try to match her voice to the image in my mind. But I can't remember anything. I keep repeating *Love you darling, Love you darling*, over and over, as I rock myself to sleep.

The phone may be old, battered, covered in grime, but when your loved ones are thousands of miles away it's a lifeline.

I realise how little I have left in my life to look forward to. Just a few minutes each day of keeping in touch. Touch?

I'm covered in cold sweat. I can hear my teeth chatter. I regret not having said what I wanted to say. But there is always another day. As I sink deeper into despair a loud bang startles me, almost throwing me off my bed. It 6.30pm. The doors have only just now been opened. I have just dreamt of being in touch with my loved one, which shows just how out of touch I am with myself.

by Anon

Granda's Last Day At Work*

I'm going to visit Granda today. It's his last day at work. He's just come back from his final mission.

Granda works for the Queen and the secret service. His job is to stop terrorists doing bad things. His work is guarded with a high fence, to stop anyone getting in. Before me and my mum can get inside the waiters – they're the men in the white shirts – have to give us a health check to make sure we don't take in any bugs or germs. They ask us to go through a big X-ray machine to check our hearts and brains, and then they pat my mum down to make sure she's not getting fat. Finally, she has to take her shoes off, so they can check that her toenails aren't too long.

Granda can't get up and play with me today as he's very tired after coming back from his mission. But when he's not on a mission we have great fun. We go into the soft play area and Granda shows me some of the moves he uses when he is arresting terrorists, and then we go and play on the computers. My favourite game is FIFA 15 and I always beat Granda. I love coming to see Granda. When he comes in, I always run up and give him a big hug. Then we go to the machines and get *Maltesers* and *Quavers* and juice. I love working the machines.

Granda and all the other soldiers have always got their uniforms on. It's got the name of his regiment on the front; HMP, which means, *Her Majesty's Protectors*. The waiters in the white shirts do all the work for the soldiers. They cook my Granda's meals and do his washing. One time we came the regiment were having a Halloween party and I dressed up as a vampire and scared all the waiters.

---

*   Based on the stories I tell my young grandchildren to hide the fact that I'm in prison.

I love it when my Granda tells me about his missions. Where he works there are loads of underground tunnels that go all around the world. Granda goes out with his men and pulls the bad terrorists down into these tunnels, then brings them back to the Queen. Then the Queen brainwashes them and makes them good people again.

Granda says when his work is finished here, he's going to take me and my cousin on a special mission. We're going to go camping and hunting for food. Granda is going to show us how to make a bow and arrow and show us how to catch rabbits and fish. I can't wait.

When the visit is finished I hug Granda dead hard and tell him he's very brave. I ask him if he knows where he will end up next. But Granda says that's him retired now.

by Eddie Mc